Coordinating art across the primary school

THE SUBJECT LEADER'S HANDBOOKS

Series Editor: Mike Harrison, Centre for Primary Education,
School of Education, The University of Manchester,
Oxford Road, Manchester, M13 9DP

Coordinating mathematics across the primary school
Tony Brown

Coordinating English at Key Stage 1
Mick Waters and Tony Martin

Coordinating English at Key Stage 2
Mick Waters and Tony Martin

Coordinating science across the primary school
Lynn D. Newton and Douglas P. Newton

Coordinating information technology across the primary school
Mike Harrison

Coordinating art across the primary school
Robert Clement, Judith Piotrowski and Ivy Roberts

Coordinating design and technology across the primary school
Alan Cross

Coordinating geography across the primary school
John Halocha

Coordinating history across the primary school
Julie Davies and Jason Redmond

Coordinating music across the primary school
Sarah Hennessy

Coordinating religious education across the primary school
Derek Bastide

Coordinating physical education across the primary school
Carole Raymond

Management skills for SEN coordinators
Sylvia Phillips, Jennifer Goodwin and Rosita Heron

Building a whole school assessment policy
Mike Wintle and Mike Harrison

The curriculum coordinator and the OFSTED inspection
Phil Gadsby and Mike Harrison

Coordinating the curriculum in the smaller primary school
Mick Waters

Coordinating art across the primary school

Robert Clement, Judith Piotrowski and Ivy Roberts

UK	RoutlegeFalmer, 11 New Fetter Lane, London EC4P 4EE
USA	RoutledgeFalmer, Taylor & Francis Inc., 29 West 35th Street, New York NY 10001

First published in 1998 by The Falmer Press

Transferred to Digital Printing 2002

RoutledgeFalmer is an imprint of the Taylor & Francis Group

A catalogue record for this book is available from the British Library

ISBN 0 7507 0695 3   paper

Library of Congress Cataloging-in-Publication Data are available on request

Jacket design by Carla Turchini

Typeset in 10/14pt by
Graphicraft Typesetters Ltd., Hong Kong

Printed and bound in Great Britain by
TJI Digital, Padstow, Cornwall

Contents

Part one
The role of the art coordinator

Part two
What art coordinators need to know

Part three
Whole school policies and schemes of work

Part four
Monitoring for quality

Part five
Resources

List of figures

Acknowledgments

The authors and publisher are grateful to the following schools and LEAs for permission to use illustrations of children's work and extracts from schools and LEA policy documents as listed below:

Chaddlewood First School, Plympton
- Documenting progression in drawing

St Michael's C of E Primary School, Kingsteignton
- Aims of the Art Handbook
- Statements of intent and objectives
- Learning experiences offered in Art

St Johns R.C. Primary School, Tiverton
- Self-evaluation profile

Stoke Hill First School, Exeter
- Illustrations of paintings and drawings of figures from Reception and Years 1, 2 and 3

Stuart Road Primary School, Plymouth
- Outline Schemes for Work in Art, Key Stage 2
- Curriculum Mapping for Art: Key Stage 2, Years 3/4
- Curriculum planning framework: Year 2, 'Kings and Queens'
- Developing painting skills
- Developing line, shape and form, texture and pattern Key Stage 1
- Organisation for painting lessons

Thornbury Primary School, Plymouth
- Illustrations of children's work for a Year 2 project on the themes of 'Degas' Dancers' and a Year 6 design based project based on the work of William Morris
- Example of the pro-forma for the Drawing Profile used in the school and illustrations from the Drawing Profile 'Seated Figures from Observation'
- Recommended organisation for the teaching of painting
- Outline of themes for work in Art: Reception to Year 6
- Balance in range of media and experiences
- The management of materials

John Bowden, Senior Art Adviser, North Yorkshire LEA
- Summary of sections usually included in school/s art policies from 'Writing an Art Policy and Curriculum Plan for a Primary School' published by AAIAD 1996, edited by John Bowden

Barking and Dagenham LEA
- Examples of End of Key Stage descriptions of achievement
- Guidance for teaching Art visual elements in Key Stage 2

Devon Curriculum Advice: Planning for Progression in Art and design
- Practices and materials for drawing

Durham LEA: Guidelines for the Implementation of Art in the National Curriculum
- Drawing Key Stages 1 and 2

East Sussex: Handbook for Art and Design in the Primary School
- Painting Key Stage 2

Essex LEA: Art and Design Curriculum Handbook
- Individual Planning Sheet
- Example of pupil's record card used to assess achievement at the end of year

Somerset LEA: Primary Art and Design, A Framework and Programmes of Study
- Planning schedule for Art focus within a topic
- Activity: Drawing KS1, Summary diagram

Series editor's preface

This book has been prepared for primary teachers charged
with the responsibility of acting as coordinators for the art
curriculum within their schools. It forms part of a series of
new publications that set out to advise such teachers on the
complex issues of improving teaching and learning through
managing each element of the primary school curriculum.

Why is there a need for such a series? Most authorities
recognise, after all, that the quality of the primary children's
work and learning depends upon the skills of their class
teacher, not in the structure of management systems, policy
documents or the titles and job descriptions of staff. Many
today recognise that school improvement equates directly to
the improvement of teaching so surely all tasks, other than
imparting subject knowledge, are merely a distraction for the
committed primary teacher.

Nothing should take teachers away from their most important
role, that is, serving the best interests of the class of children
in their care and this book, and the others in the series, does
not wish to diminish that mission. However, the increasing
complexity of the primary curriculum and society's expanding
expectations, makes it very difficult for the class teacher to
keep up to date with every development. Within traditional
subject areas there has been an explosion of knowledge and
new fields introduced such as science, technology, design,
problem solving and health education, not to mention the uses

of computers. These are now considered entitlements for primary children. Furthermore, we now expect all children to succeed at these studies, not just the fortunate few. All this has overwhelmed a class teacher system largely unchanged since the inception of primary schools.

Primary class teachers cannot possibly be an expert in every aspect of the curriculum they are required to teach. To whom can they turn for help? It is unrealistic to assume that such support will be available from the headteacher whose responsibilities have grown ever wider since the 1988 Educational Reform Act. Constraints, including additional staff costs, and the loss of benefits from the strength and security of the class teacher system, militate against wholesale adoption of specialist or semi-specialist teaching. Help therefore has to come from exploiting the talents of teachers themselves, in a process of mutual support. Hence primary schools have chosen many and varied systems of consultancy or subject coordination which best suit the needs of their children and the current expertise of the staff.

In fact, curriculum leadership functions in primary schools have increasingly been shared with class teachers through the policy of curriculum coordination for the past twenty years, especially to improve the consistency of work in language and mathematics. Since then each school has developed their own system and the series recognises that the one each reader is part of will be a compromise between the ideal and the possible. Campbell and Neill (1994) show that by 1991 nearly nine out of every ten primary class teachers had such responsibility and the average number of subjects each was between 1.5 and 2.2 (depending on the size of school).

These are the people for whom this series sets out to help to do this part of their work. The books each deal with specific issues whilst at the same time providing an overview of general themes in the management of the subject curriculum. The term *subject leader* is used in an inclusive sense and combines the two major roles that such teachers play when they have responsibility for subjects and aspects of the primary curriculum.

The books each deal with:

■ coordination — a role which emphasises harmonising, bringing together, making links, establishing routines and common practice; and

■ subject leadership — a role which emphasises; providing information, offering expertise and direction, guiding the development of the subject, and raising standards.

The purpose of the series is to give practical guidance and support to teachers in particular what to do and how to do it. They each offer help on the production, development and review of policies and schemes of work; the organisation of resources, and developing strategies for improving the management of the subject curriculum.

Each book in the series contains material that subject managers will welcome and find useful in developing their subject expertise and in tackling problems of enthusing and motivating staff.

Each book has five parts.

1 The review and development of the different roles coordinators are asked to play.
2 Updating subject knowledge and subject pedagogical knowledge.
3 Developing and maintaining policies and schemes of work.
4 Monitoring work within the school to enhance the continuity of teaching and progression in pupil's learning.
5 Resources and contacts.

Although written primarily for teachers who are art coordinators, Judith, Ivy and Bob offer practical guidance and many ideas for anyone in the school who has a responsibility for the art curriculum including teachers with an overall role in coordinating the whole or key stage curriculum and the deputy head and the headteacher.

In making the book easily readable the writers have drawn upon their considerable experience as a teacher educators, researchers and art specialists. The combination of three enthusiasts, each with their own perspectives on primary art has led to invaluable advice to those attempting to develop a whole-school view of progress in art education, particularly those who are new to the job or have recently changed schools. It will help readers develop both the subject expertise they will need and the managerial perspective necessary to enthuse others. This is most pertinent at a time when some threaten primary children with an ever narrowing curriculum in an attempt to raise test scores. Art coordinators will need the skills and knowledge outlined in this book to keep art alive in primary classrooms.

Mike Harrison, Series Editor
February 1998

Part one · The role of the art coordinator

Chapter 1

The role of the art coordinator

There are many diverse routes to becoming the art coordinator — it could be that you didn't step back quickly enough when the head was asking for volunteers or it may be that you are a well-qualified and enthusiastic soul who applied for the job and passed the searching interview. There is the bi-polar continuum of suitability for the post and you will know your own position and valence upon it! Wherever you are there will probably be a lot to do. The National Curriculum in Art (hereafter NC Art) is a document which is brimming with good practice and high expectations. While this was what was needed it can highlight a mismatch between the coordinator's vision and that of colleagues who are coping with other equally demanding non-core foundation subjects as well.

Let's consider the inspection findings relating to the co-ordination of art in primary schools. The following are the key issues for schools taken from the OFSTED inspections report 1995,

Key issues for primary schools

- To meet the full National Curriculum requirements schools need to provide a broad and balanced art curriculum that includes two and three-dimensional work and addresses the two attainment targets, and to provide sufficient resources for this to be achieved.

- Good teaching in art is best supported by sound planning which provides for the progressive acquisition and reinforcement of skills. Teachers need to have a clear idea of what constitutes good standards in art, and to have high expectations of their pupils; these should be communicated by direct instruction, through discussion and through the display of art in schools. This will support improved preparation for art activities by individual teachers.

- Much can be achieved where an art coordinator has sufficient subject expertise. Schools should ensure that the coordinator has appropriate training and opportunities to influence the development of the subject throughout the school.

Unsurprisingly then, OFSTED highlight the need for careful planning that includes an orchestrated approach to assessment and recording and the coordinator's subject knowledge. You will find reference to these issues throughout this book with specific, detailed consideration given as follows:

- subject knowledge — Part 2
- planning — Part 3
- assessment — Part 4

As coordinator you will be wise to set up a framework for both the regular review of art education in your school and a framework for any changes necessary. These needn't be mutually exclusive. Such a framework for review would include the following elements:

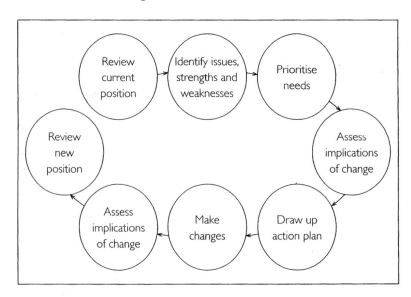

The process above is most effectively achieved when it is an experience shared with colleagues. That said, you need to have done your homework before consulting with colleagues — it's one thing to work with colleagues, it's another to get them to do it for you (or to you, if you've gone in unprepared!). Never go in to a discussion about reviewing art education in your school without having your own perceptions ready for scrutiny. Have your own approach clear in your own mind before you throw the agenda open to others. Harrison (1998) provides a useful framework for working with colleagues.

Review your current position

One of the first tasks you will face as the appointed art coordinator is the formulation of evidence of where your school is currently at in its development of art education. There are a variety of ways in which you could proceed and it is probably the eclectic approach that will work best. Pathways to clarifying the current status include:

How to review the current provision:

read the school policy on art if it exists;
read the schemes of work for art;
examine the schools long- and medium-term plans for art;
look at existing collections of children's work, e.g. samples kept for Ofsted inspections;
look at current record keeping;
investigate the system for resourcing the art curriculum;
consider Inset provision for art over the previous five years;
discover the particular facilities offered by your school for art education.

The above can form a checklist for you in the early days and will help to prioritise the demands upon your time. If the policy is well written and the schemes of work reflect those stated intentions then you may well turn your attention to planning, assessment, recording and resourcing. So having looked at the above list of evidence you can now evaluate each of the following major issues using the pragmatic headings of status and response.

Review of:	Status	Response
Policy	there is already an effective policy which clarifies purpose, provision and practice	it will need annual review
Policy	no policy written	contact local authority for framework policy and use in accordance with guidelines in Chapter 9 of this book
Staff	enthusiastic skilled	support by good programme of training and support — see Chapter 2 in this book
Staff	few art skills to draw upon, inadequate or no training programme	identify any good practice and organise staff training — see p. 14 in Chapter 2.
Resources	good range of media represented, well maintained, efficient access	maintain and update ensure provision for: dry and wet *and* 2D and 3D
Resources	limited, poorly housed, inefficient access	secure appropriate funding, identify needs from medium term plans/schemes of work, use basic shopping list in Chapter 15
Headteacher's attitude	informed financial support given, encouraging, sees art work as an expression of the quality of provision at the school	reward your head with: a well written policy, well-resourced art curriculum, well-organised staff training, school wide demonstrations of children's achievements
Headteacher's attitude	art has low priority	you need to secure: a budget (list in Chapter 15), Inset time, the support of head — use Ofsted reports that describe the positive influence of heads and be sure that you adopt a positive approach
Planning	detailed schemes of work ensuring progression, continuity — planning for art is shared with parents	set targets for evaluation of the effectiveness of the planning in terms of teaching and learning outcomes and efficiency
Planning	minimal	*short-term response:* you draft schemes of work for each year group using planning sheet B from Non-Statutory Guidance (NSG) or similar/use local authority schemes of work *medium-term response:* you will work with year group teachers to produce medium- and short-term plans directly related to long-term plans and overall policy *long-term response:* teachers will recommend improvements to planning in the light of experience
Monitoring, assessment, recording, reporting and accountability.	cohesive programme of well-planned assessments of children's achievements	maintain and improve good practice: moderation across year groups, exemplar materials from your school in a file alongside those provided by SCAA, recording and reporting to children and parents in a variety of ways.
Monitoring, assessment, recording, reporting and accountability.	minimal	see recommendations in Part 4 of this book

You can add your own key issues, e.g. quality of teaching is a critical issue and one where you will need to develop the trust of the staff before you can evaluate it. Another issue might be accommodation, perhaps you can see ways of rationalising space, store rooms and maybe even classrooms. All the above could equally be presented individually on a continuum of extremes from left to right and you could set targets and monitor development (see action plan that follows). You may find that you are in the fortunate position of maintaining, monitoring and improving existing good provision gradually.

Equally you may find that you need to be the instigator of a range of rapid changes. A clear vision of these targets presented with straightforward documentation will help you in your initial discussions with your head regarding the schedule you propose.

The above should help you to arrive at an action plan. Such a plan should identify short-, medium- and long-term targets.

Prioritise needs

Having considered the current provision and identified key issues and responses you will need to prioritise. This will be influenced by the timescale available to you. For example, if your appointment follows a recent OFSTED inspection the chances are that priorities are already identified and that you can reasonably count on having four years to put your vision into effect. In such a scenario it follows that you will have:

■ the opportunity to plan for a programme of INSET/training;
■ time to consult with staff;
■ you will be able to consider the whole school long-term plans and related schemes of work;
■ carry out an analysis of existing resources;
■ develop a policy;
■ arrive at a coherent plan for assessment and monitoring;
■ establish yourself in the role of art coordinator;
■ and gain the trust and respect of your colleagues.

Alternatively, you may be appointed art coordinator with a short time scale for the above and judicious prioritisation of needs will be necessary. Your commitment to developing all aspects of policy will inevitably be compromised by the urgent need for action. Your priorities will need to be:

■ write a policy — use local authority framework;
■ write schemes of work — use planning sheet B in NSG for medium-term plans and Chapter 9;
■ write a statement of intent regarding monitoring, assessment, recording, reporting and accountability — use Part 4 for good practice on this and your local authority guidelines;
■ record your proposals for INSET/training;

■ write a statement on resources with costing and an overall budget — use Chapter 15 for this.

Assess implications of change

Before forging ahead with the writing of your action plan you will need to reflect on the possible implications of the changes that you have in mind at both professional and interpersonal levels. You will need to consider:

■ teaching style favoured by your staff — is there a proper policy or simply an accepted common approach to teaching strategy in your school? (e.g. interactive whole class, group work or individual) How would your vision fit with this and how could you enable staff to accommodate the changes that your vision might involve? For example, can you organise for other staff to observe you? INSET time used for visits to well-chosen schools?

■ existing practice in planning — is your vision of planning contrary to this? For example, your school may operate a top down model wherein the coordinator structures the framework for planning for progression and continuity and the year group teachers subsequently work with the coordinator to develop schemes of work. Alternatively, your school may operate a bottom up approach wherein, for example, the coordinator would first work with colleagues to establish their desires regarding what to teach in each year group and then the coordinator builds these pieces of planning into a cohesive plan for teaching and learning ensuring continuity and progression;

■ existing demands on colleagues and children for monitoring, assessment, recording, reporting and accountability (MARRA) — how do your proposals fit with these? Typically, most schools will commit a far greater amount of time and effort to addressing MARRA for English and mathematics, but understandably less for the remaining subjects;

■ resources — will your approach to the ordering, storage, distribution and maintenance of resources be different from previous practice? If you predict that there may be some initial resistance to your new style, then you may need to temper the process of change with, for example, self-deprecating humour (before and after photographs of your own stock room or classroom sink area) or sheer hard graft (you organise the lifting and shifting of the heavy/awkward paper supplies). The point is made elsewhere in this chapter that colleagues are usually prepared to forgive a lot in the face of sheer enthusiasm and energy;

- interpersonal awareness — will there be any implications for the responsibilities of other colleagues resulting from the process of change you propose? You will need to ameliorate some of the potential interpersonal difficulties by appraising colleagues with related interests of the changes, rather than treading on toes. Be aware of where your responsibilities and resources impinge on someone else's. It can make the difference between developing shared understandings and profitable working approaches on the one hand and negative tensions, duplication of work and an undermining of purposeful endeavour on the other. For example, have you appraised the Key Stage 2 coordinator of your proposal to purchase sketch books as the money for this may come out of their budget? Is there a planning or assessment coordinator for the school — appraise them of specific implications of change. You may be about to introduce a lot of 'wet and messy' art activities where previously there has been an overemphasis on dry observational drawing — this will probably have some implications for the caretaker and will the school provide art overalls or will parents need to provide an art shirt for each child?

- the tone you adopt will have a significant effect on the way in which your message of change is received. Will you be serious and enthusiastic about the job or pompous and officious? Are you able to identify tensions and discuss difficulties or will you only listen to positive comments from supportive colleagues? When things go awry will you adopt a pragmatic approach to sort out the crisis and learn lessons subsequently, rather than to overtly apportion blame? To be an effective coordinator you will need to accommodate the shortcomings of some colleagues and the potential of others. Accepting and understanding the way people are is an important first step to being able to get the most out of them.

Draw up an action plan

You will need to draw up an action plan whatever the particulars of your context. You have already reviewed current position, identified issues, prioritised needs and assessed the implications of change. You need to present your action plan in a clear user-friendly format and the following is an example that may help structure your proposals.

Key Issue 1: Development of policy for art

Issues/objectives	Action	Personnel	Time-scale	Resources	Targets — Success criteria	Monitoring, evaluation
1.1 To initiate the formulation of a policy for art	Coordinator evaluates current position	Coordinator, year group staff	Autumn term	Time — supply cover for four separate half days: £240	A statement of current provision identifying: time analysis; balance; coherence and progression; links with other subjects; resources; A,R&R; staff expertise.	Review at staff meeting
1.2 To produce a draft policy for art	Coordinator to produce the policy in agreement with year group staff using the LA framework document in the first instance	Coordinator, year group staff	Spring term	Time — year group meetings — four half days supply cover: £240	Draft document to present to staff in Summer term	Circulated for comment to senior staff
1.3 To present the draft policy to all staff for final amendments	Coordinator to use staff meeting to present and discuss the draft policy	Coordinator, all staff	Final staff meeting, Spring term	Time	An agreed art policy	Feed-back from all staff to be reviewed by coordinator

Repeat for each key issue.

Your action plan will need a supporting statement to give a rationale for the action that you are proposing but keep it brief and use simple, direct language to maximise impact and acceptance.

Chapter 2

Establishing yourself in the role of art coordinator

Coordinators can sometimes be so aware of not wanting
to appear threatening or officious to colleagues that they
actually hold themselves back from being business-like and
professional. In terms of your initial approaches to the job you
will need to remind yourself that long-standing colleagues will
forgive your attentions as the assumption of responsibility for
art (they will be probably be glad that someone is doing it), if
on the other hand you are new to the school assume that
colleagues are impressed by your enthusiasm and efficiency.

You will need to:
■ establish and develop both the role of art coordinator for
  your school and yourself as the person within that role;
■ be the interpreter of the NC — its intentions, aims and
  practical implications for teaching and learning. Keep in
  touch with your local adviser for art and attend updating
  sessions;
■ be the interpreter and disseminator of related official
  publications — e.g. Non-statutory Guidance, OFSTED
  checklists for inspection criteria, assessment issues;
■ put art on the conscious agenda of the school — physically
  and mentally;
■ be honest about what you bring to the role — you may not
  have a degree in fine art but you *do* know the detail of NC
  Art *and* you have developed your skills in art through
  training *and* you are constantly developing your subject
  knowledge (see Part 2);

- shape or reshape the policy;
- support other staff;
- involve the parents — does your school send A4 medium-term planning sheets home to parents at the end of the previous half-term so they know what lies ahead? If not, why don't you start the ball rolling? In the plethora of dull things that are sent home to parents, many schools still fail to send the one thing that parents crave: knowledge of what are the teachers are teaching, and how can parents help/augment the learning process. Make sure your 'garden' is less secret and more tended and shared!

Practical approaches to fulfilling your role as art coordinator

There are various ways in which all coordinators can work effectively to improve provision for their subject. These are usefully described by Harrison (1998). Some of these are highly visible such as producing a timetable for development through INSET or reporting to governors' meetings. Others are more subtle and supportive, such as working alongside colleagues, the demonstration of particular techniques, or by the example of their own practice with their class. The ordering and storage of materials is, done well, an almost invisible aspect of your work, but a crucial one. The materials you and your colleagues order will shape and be shaped by the fundamental purposes of your intentions, aims, planning and assessment strategy.

One of the most useful things you can do to develop your policy for art education in your school is to contact your local authority for their framework policy for art. These are usually very good and mean that you don't have to reinvent the wheel. Don't assume that a framework policy won't fit your school — equally be aware that at least some modification will be necessary to reflect the particulars of your school.

Remember that these are useful guidelines with structure and format to ensure that you demonstrate how your school will fulfil the intentions of NC Art. At their best, these framework policies will support the development of your school's art policy by structuring the issues that you and your colleagues need to address (aims, statement of compliance with NC Art, statements on planning for all children, teaching strategies, assessment, recording and reporting, staffing and staff development, funding and resourcing, and evaluation and review of policy).

Particularly good examples of such framework policies include those produced by East Sussex, Somerset, Durham, Stockport, Bolton and Bury. These framework policies often have related documents which will further inform the detail of schemes of work e.g. Bury's 'Art — a list of skills' document is strongly recommended. A full consideration of policies for art can be found in Chapter 9.

Having drawn up your action plan you should have determined your tasks. You need to map these out in terms of:

■ issues which can be dealt with by memo, e.g. checking availability/location of resources or inviting response to the product of a training day — 'These are my notes from our planning for art day, have I missed anything? Please comment!' or 'This is the policy so far, thanks for all the inputs — please comment.';

■ issues which can be addressed by a simple questionnaire (more appropriate in a large school), these can be used as hard copy evidence for OFSTED of one way in which you monitor the effectiveness of your policy (remember if it's not written down, it's not happening!!);

■ issues which need no more than perhaps a five minute slice of a staff meeting in which to alert colleagues to an initial phase of review (e.g. of resources, of policy) 'I'm going to be collecting/visiting/asking opinions about . . .';

■ and issues that will require half or full INSET days, e.g. a thorough review of art provision, completely new policy formulation, presentation of schemes of work for the whole school combined with skills or subject knowledge training.

You will need to establish a two year cycle of development within the available INSET programme for art. Be precise and book half or full day slots for these. Check the cycle of review for art within the staff-meeting programme — when is art due for some time in the weekly programme? Typically this might be in the after-school-on-Monday slot.

Staff development

You are now in a position to know your priorities and the modes through which you will approach those priorities. You will need to plan out a timetable with your headteacher for staff development in art to cover major new initiatives (new/revised schemes of work, new policy, new ways of working, e.g. artists in school), a detailed consideration of MARRA, including exemplification of standards (your own school's and those materials provided by SCAA, 1997) and the development of art skills and subject knowledge. Such a day will often include consideration of resources — allow time for this as well.

INSET — running it, organising it, initiating change and reaffirming philosophy

Having weighed the evidence it will benefit both your development and that of the children's art education if you arrange some INSET time for art. Aim for a whole day but accept half a day! It is vital that you maximise the use of this time and don't give all your art INSET over to an outside speaker. Where you can use outside speakers effectively is when they combine their role as speaker with that of impartial facilitator, i.e. they not only input but present and use a framework to generate output as well. Details of planning for effective INSET are given in this chapter but it is relevant here to consider the substance of a major aspect of your discussions with your colleagues — the shared understanding of the purposes of art education.

There are five essential features of an effective INSET training day:
1 clarity of purpose
2 good level of communication and organisation before the event and on the day
3 an outcome to be achieved
4 useful, documented follow up
5 an appropriate satisfaction factor

Clarity of purpose

This should have come from your earlier work on identifying priorities and sorting out the appropriate medium of communication for these. Be sure that you know the purpose (obvious) and the mode of operating (not always considered) e.g. is this training half day/day going to be used for sharing understandings to formulate the policy, brainstorming for fleshing out the schemes of work to ensure continuity and progression of skills development, or for training in particular art skills for all staff? Each will require a different pace, tone and setting.

If the INSET is going to be used for the dissemination of, say, schemes of work then you need to be sure that the tone is evaluative, not simply descriptive. The schemes of work or the policy document should be distributed beforehand, summarised on the day (e.g. using OHP) and referred to for insights and criticism.

Good levels of communication and organisation before the event and on the day

- you have booked this INSET time with the head well in advance and it has been included in the INSET timetable;
- you have clarified and published precise times for start/lunch/finish (I once did an inservice day in a school where different members of staff had been given different start times by their coordinator, ranging from 8.30am to 9.30am!)
- you have prepared a timetable/agenda for the INSET so everyone is
  - (a) aware of how well organised you are (never a bad thing) and
  - (b) everyone is well aware of the importance, significance and purpose you attach to the INSET;
- as you have already decided on the purpose of the INSET by prioritising needs and discussing these with colleagues informally and briefly, perhaps in staff meetings, you should be in a position to communicate the purpose(s) of the INSET;
- communicate all the above in final version in writing — confusion can ensue when details are only communicated orally;

- if the notion of a pack of documentation for an INSET day is relatively novel in your school then present one — colour code the contents and make an impact. People find enthusiasm hard to ignore and even harder to criticise. If, on the other hand, colleagues are fed up with 'course packs' then go for something completely different — theme your paperwork and keep it to a minimum, stagger it over the session, anything to make sure that both the content and import of the day is attended to and easily recalled;

- as you are the art coordinator/manager you may wish to consider some minor details of presentation of paperwork, e.g. print the agenda/plan of the day on cartridge paper, use colour effectively — reinforce and enhance visual literacy at every opportunity!

- who needs to know about the INSET — will you need to summarise the provision for the governors or the impending inspection team? If so, do it straightaway — write it down!

- are you booking an outside speaker/craftsperson? Book them as soon as you can and put it in writing, including a statement of the fee, and keep their reply. Equally, remember to write nearer the time, reaffirming the booking and the scope/purpose of the day. You will, of course, have discussed your needs over the 'phone but you will need to put all that in writing. Confirm their needs both dietary (e.g. they only drink elderflower tea with goats' milk) and professional (e.g. they'll need to display children's work, a big table, a flip-chart, a video, a tape recorder and/or, worse, a slide projector!)

An outcome to be achieved

What are the learning outcomes for the INSET?

Are they tangible, e.g. a successfully redrafted policy, transformed schemes of work, an exciting new approach to i.e. MARRA, complete with documentation?

Or are they intangible, e.g. enhanced understanding of the intentions of NC Art, practical experiences of assessment moderation, encouraging colleagues to feel confident in their own responses to art work, developing use of the language of art?

Maybe it will be skills based, e.g. a practical skills training session on use of clay, drawing, printing, using and manipulating digitised images using cameras and computers . . .

Consider the reality of what you are aiming for and resource it accordingly. You can't run an INSET day on using the work of other artists with children without getting hold of some stimulating artefacts for your INSET. You can't expect colleagues to write the proposed documentation for you so come ready — circulate your proposals beforehand or at least your comments on the relevant issues, however nascent!

Useful documented follow-up

Having worked so hard, had so many heated discussions, and had so many ideas proposed and dashed, it is a good idea to keep notes and to use these to confirm/summarise agreements and action points after the INSET. Part of the day should be to consider 'Where next?' and it is important not to lose the momentum of the enthusiasm from the experience. Write it down and circulate it.

Evaluate the day honestly and set out the resulting action, recommendations, proposals. Include the discussed resource implications and plans for how funding might be achieved. Circulate the results.

Evaluate the participants' satisfaction with the day

So far in this section the points made refer largely to the professional issues that are the major part of the INSET you are planning. There are additional dimensions to INSET arrangements, e.g. they are rare and precious occasions for teachers to be exclusively in adult company at work, they are a useful team building opportunity, they are an opportunity for you to establish yourself as the person responsible for art and as a competent colleague.

You need to be sure that you accommodate these points in your planning of the day.

■ After all that intensive debate, how have you rewarded your colleagues — at break times, at lunch times?

- Did you secure a budget from your headteacher for refreshments?
- Do other professions all have to bring a dish of something for lunch on their training days?
- Don't your colleagues deserve a decent cup of coffee?
- Was the room arranged/heated/ventilated appropriately?
- Did you provide pens, paper etc. to make life easier for your colleagues?
- Did you arrange with the cleaners to dust and vacuum clean that room first so that it was ready for you from, say, 8am?
- Did you arrange for the secretary to take all calls and only to interrupt for life and death emergencies?
- If the secretary is involved in the whole staff INSET, have you arranged for a parent to be at the 'phone so that you are not constantly losing a member of staff?
- Interruptions are an indicator of the esteem — or lack of it — in which the proceedings are held.

I can recall vividly the astonishment of one coordinator when at 11.30am on an INSET day the headteacher stood up and announced that he was just off to take the dog to be shorn!

As stated earlier, there are resource implications in terms of time and funding if colleagues are to have opportunities to develop their own skills. Having established the need for colleagues to have practical experience during inservice days, what is the best way forward?

Concentrate on what is achievable in your INSET. Initially, it is important that colleagues participate successfully and take pleasure in their work. Depending on the needs, attitudes and interests that you have identified amongst your colleagues, decide a starting point. A theme such as natural forms (shells, bones, dried seaweed); a local landmark (railway station, airport, mill) can be a useful unifying focus, but for a staff predominantly peopled by the nervous, more precise nurturing and guidance is necessary at first. Where this is the case, begin with non-threatening activities:

- look closely, perhaps through a viewfinder, at the arrangement of lines which create pattern and texture on a natural surface such as wood, feathers etc.;
- make small sketchbook studies of samples;

- encourage your colleagues to examine shapes, colours and tones through the viewfinder, without putting pressure on them to make accurate maps of what they see;
- let them enjoy scaling up these small studies and turning them into large abstract paintings with the emphasis on exploring shape and colour rather than insisting on a recognisable image.

It is as much your role to lead your colleagues to achievable ends in this context as it is for all teachers to set a context in which pupils are safe to experiment, experience success and identify development points.

The following are examples of practical workshops which you could use as a basis for planning your own INSET.

Workshop 1: Exploring National Curriculum Art (see also Clark, 1995)

Strands 7c and 7e provide a useful focus for discussion in initiating critical dialogue. The programmes of study state what pupils should be taught and it is clearly crucial that teachers know what is meant by pattern, texture, colour, line, tone, shape, form and space so that they can engage in meaningful and critical discussion with pupils and colleagues about their work, development, progression and about the work of other artists. Initial discussion to clarify terms and meanings is necessary but this discussion must be supported by practical application through the workshops and, if possible, gallery visits.

Where there is shared understanding and agreement about the language and objectives of the NC in art, colleagues will readily perceive the superficial and non-challenging nature of activities and tasks that are sometimes offered to children in the guise of 'art and craft'. Specifically I am referring to mass-produced greeting cards, seasonal scenes involving small pieces of screwed-up tissue paper, much labour and no learning, templates to be drawn around and the shapes 'coloured in' and so on. It is clearly important to be sensitive in leading this discussion and to remember and stress that most of us have at some stage involved ourselves and our pupils in activities where learning and process have taken second place to product. We need to be honest about this, and move on.

The following chart gives some indication of initial activities which can be used to explore the visual elements of art, and some brief suggestions about artists whose work can be used to exemplify the concepts.

Headings are: TERMS. BRIEF INDICATION OF SOME ACTIVITIES. ARTISTS.

Line/shape
Experiments (in sketchbooks) with different mark-making tools to explore straight lines, curves, different thickness, zigzags, crayon resist, IT, circles, triangles, rectangles, printing with shapes (e.g. shapes in nature, shapes in buildings), cutting and overlaying shapes.
Miro, Klee, Mondrian, Picasso, Kandinsky, Chinese, Egyptian, African art

Colour/tone
Primary colours, secondary colours, colour wheels, sorting tones, mixing, matching, coloured shapes, overlaying tissue papers, colour in nature, colour in landscape, tones in paintings, recognising and setting colour.
Monet, Gaugin, Seurat, Mondrian, Matisse, Van Gogh, Klimt, O'Keeffe, Rousseau, Aboriginal art

Texture

Clay, sand, wool, wood, sandpaper, scrim, rubbings, small sample drawings, card, batik, weaving, leaves, feathers, paper-making, sorting textures — rough/smooth.

Goldsworthy, Palozzi, O'Keeffe, Sutherland

Pattern

Pattern in nature, link with shape studies, repeat prints with found objects, symmetrical patterns, lino and press printing.

O'Keeffe, William Morris, Islamic tiles, Roman mosaics, Aboriginal art

Form/space

Sorting spheres, cubes, bricks, other solids, curled paper, papier mâché, clay tiles, sculptures using found objects, modroc, masks. 2D into 3D.

Giacommetti, Rodin, Moore, Goldsworthy, Hepworth, Nicholson, Picasso, African art, masks in different cultures

This chart suggests starting points but is by no means exhaustive. It might help in the generation of discussion about planning throughout the school to meet National Curriculum requirements and an effective scheme of work for art.

Workshop 2: Batik Painting

A good idea is to focus on a particular skill or process for the workshop day, and through this identify the visual elements that will be explored and other artists whose work lends support. A day spent batik painting, for example, is always popular and need not be threatening. Through the activity, colleagues will be working with textiles and exploring line, shape, colour, texture, tone and possibly space and pattern. It will already be part of most teachers' experience to have used wax resist with their children, using crayon, paper and paint. This day will add to the interest and excitement of wax resist and, provided that health and safety needs are observed, it is a skill that teachers can share with their children.

You will need

- Tjanting tools. These are the special tools with brass or copper nozzles of varying thickness which are used to pour the heated wax onto fabric. Choose concorde shaped tools with front-pouring nozzles. Side pourers disadvantage left-handed people;
- Wax. Blocks or granules can be bought from many general education supply catalogues. They should be mixed in a ratio of 80% paraffin and 20% beeswax;
- Electric batik pot;
- The following colours in batik dye or brusho (easibrush). The main ones are underlined.
  brilliant yellow, navy, red, yellow, brilliant blue, black
  olive green, red-brown, turquoise.
- Cartridge paper, pencil and black felt tip pen;
- Drawing pins and a wooden frame if possible per person;
- Untreated cotton fabric;
- A large tub of dye for the final dip (unless the whole work is to be painted);
- Hot iron and kitchen paper.

Preparation

Assemble the equipment with protective sheets on all surfaces.
- Switch on the pots and melt the wax.

- Check that the fabric absorbs the dye and the wax. If it rejects either the results will be disappointing. This should only happen if you forgot to buy *untreated* cotton.
- Begin with small pieces of fabric and a variety of tjantings. Dip the tjanting into the hot wax. Make sure that the cup has time to reach a temperature that enables the wax to drip freely through the nozzle.
- Using a folded paper towel to catch any drips, take the tool, tip the fabric and explore through play how the unfamiliar mark-making tool works.
- As you gain confidence in using the tool and more control over the dripping wax you can move on.

Moving on from play

- Sketch a design on the cartridge paper. This could be taken from the small shape and colour samples, or, for the more adventurous, the content could be landscape, portrait, a pattern, design etc.
- Go over the design in black felt tip to create a cartoon which is then traced lightly onto the fabric using pencil.
- Stretch the fabric drum tight over the wooden frame and secure with drawing pins.
- Prepare the dyes. Depending on the purpose and the type of dye you may need carefully to follow the manufacturer's instructions about fixing. Brusho (easibrush) is cheap, easy to use and will suit most batik painting purposes in the primary school.
- Apply hot wax over the pencil marks and make sure the wax penetrates to the back of the material and does not sit on top. If this happens, either the wax is not hot enough or the wrong fabric is being used.
- Paint on cold colours.
- Allow these to dry well and apply wax to fix them.
- Paint on warm colours.
- Allow to dry and apply wax as before.
- Add further areas of colour, always allowing to dry well before applying wax to fix.
- Scratch details into the wax if necessary. If you do this, soaking in a large final tub of dye will produce the marbled effect characteristic of batik dyeing.
- Hang to dry.
- Pick off large areas of wax and iron off the rest between sheets of brown or kitchen paper.
- Batik is best displayed with the light behind it, but can be mounted by stretching over a board, hung from a cane or used in bookbinding.

Important safety points

Basic, common sense precautions need to be observed and perhaps stressed with less experienced members of staff:

- The activities need to be planned to ensure progression and the opportunities for playing and experimenting with the materials and processes in a safe, controlled environment should not be hurried.
- Only ever work with small groups of closely-supervised children when there is extra adult help available.
- *Never* leave the children or the batik pots unattended. Remove them to a separate safe place after the lesson and label them HOT.
- Be clear about the agreed school policy in respect of such equipment.
- Make sure that no leads trail on the floor.
- Have the worktable against the wall where the plug socket is.
- Keep the room well-ventilated at all times and be aware of children who may react to the slight fumes.
- Rest the pot regularly by switching off as frequently as the supplier recommends.

Batik painting has to be tried for the creative possibilities to be realised. A workshop day or days can be thoroughly enjoyable and very worthwhile. The points above can only describe the process. It is in the activities with colleagues that positive attitudes can be encouraged and achievements acknowledged.

Workshop 3: Displaying Work, Celebrating Achievement

It is rare to meet a teacher whose attitudes are so hardened that they do not ultimately respond in some measure to success through practical work and experiences which in turn bear fruit in the classroom with their pupils. Attitudes can harden in the case of teachers who are afraid of having their weaknesses exposed to ridicule. Children deserve a beautiful and wholesome environment in which to work and to see that time and care has been taken to value their work through display. The same is true of adults and their achievements on this workshop day need to be recognised.

When displaying the outcomes of the workshop, stress the importance of teachers sharing their work with each other and with their children and make sure that evidence of the learning process is included, not just the final product.

Practical points about displaying work

You need to agree a school approach to displaying work, but the following points might be useful both in displaying your workshop outcomes and in generating discussion about a school approach to display.
- Space is important in display. Pieces of work need to be linked together. Gaps between work need carefully to be considered and a flow of work maintained.
- It is often a good idea to map out the display on the floor until an acceptable arrangement is agreed. Always try to include the children in this when it is their work.
- The size of the pieces of work needs to vary. Rows and columns of A4 pieces, for example would be less visually interesting than a variety.
- The content needs to vary. Include play pieces, scribbles, cartoons which lead to the conclusion, not just the final outcome.
- Examples of books made in school can be included. (Batik covers are very effective.) Examples of commercially produced batik can be displayed alongside your own in fabric form, photographs or in books.
- Draped material can be effective in enhancing displays of work. Batik painting lends itself well to this.
- The tools used in the classroom can form part of the displays in the classroom. The room can become a workshop where each child knows the place of each item and returns it, properly cleaned, to its appointed place after use. A set of gleaming tjantings could form a very attractive, inter-active part of your workshop display.

Mounting work

- If you are including the sketches and display designs, double mounting is attractive but not essential.
- Mounting should be straight, no curly edges or pinking sheared finishes.
- The bottom margin can be wider if preferred.
- If double mounted the outer mount looks better if it is narrower than the inner mount.
- Displaying the children's work on the paper they chose is better than cutting out sections or altering/adding to it.
- Subtle subdued colours will enhance the work without drawing attention away from it.
- If in doubt use natural, white or off-white sugar paper. A thin double mount of black can be very effective.
- Work need not necessarily be glued to the backing paper. Straight pins can be used to attach the work through the mounts to the display board. The mounts can later be recycled and the work stored in a book or portfolio.
- Work is best displayed straight rather than at angles on the wall. Be guided by standards in gallery collections, to which you will ensure your colleagues have access.

The above points can be used to generate discussion both when displaying the outcomes of your day exploring batik painting and in the wider context of agreeing a policy for using the school environment to reflect and celebrate the work and achievements of the children.

Practical Workshop 4: Planning a Day with the Work of Other Artists

- A day initially spent in the familiar security of school could be one workshop for a staff of five or fewer, or a larger staff could be split into smaller groups, focusing on a variety of works.
- An initial, warm-up exercise could be to look at prints, postcards or posters of several varying works and agreeing, perhaps in pairs, which visual elements the work makes use of.
- For example, Klee's 'Coloured Lightning' 1927 exemplifies use of line, shape and colour.
- If you are able to provide plenty of varied postcards etc., pairs can share their perceptions and argue their case for suggesting that, for example, shape and colour are important elements in Klee's paintings.
- As well as initiating sustained discussion, this exercise consolidates understanding of the concepts, line, tone, colour, shape form, space, pattern and texture, and will encourage your colleagues to contribute meaningfully to discussion about progression in the scheme of work.

In the second part of the morning, discussion can move on to Taylor's framework (1992). As mentioned earlier, reference to the questions posed under the four headings, content, form, process and mood provides a sound and simple structure for discussion. It is in the area of 'content' in addition to identifying use of visual elements, that your colleagues might now need additional support.

- If you offer your colleagues a simple range of concepts to identify in looking at and engaging with artworks, you will be leading them towards an understanding of the artist through the artist's work, rather than beginning with the life history of the artist, which movement s/he belonged to and so on.
- Terms like portrait, landscape, still life, figurative, abstract, semi-abstract, provide manageable and quite probably familiar starting points to facilitate dialogue about the content of the work being studied.
- Ensure that the works you choose for this exercise exemplify these terms and your colleagues will be well on the way to enjoying, understanding and sharing the collection you have prepared for them.

The final session of the day could, in part, be an exercise in planning what to do in the medium- and long-term with the outcomes of the morning's sessions. Key questions:
- What visual elements and skills are currently being explored in each class?
- How might an understanding of other artists' work be applied?
- What cross-curricular possibilities are there?
- Could a simple framework for researching other artists be agreed, including basic details:
  Who was the artist?
  When did s/he live?
  Where did s/he live?
  When was the art made?
  Where is it now?
- The questions under the headings Form, Process and Mood (Taylor, 1992) could now be applied.

Projects to plan for in the afternoon might include:
- looking at other works by the same artist;
- identifying differences/similarities;
- identifying trends/art movements of the time;
- researching the social context of the time and so on.

These are all delights which can be developed from the starting point of this workshop and enjoyed by you, your colleagues and the children.

Helping colleagues and induction of new staff

The community of people who compose the school will inevitably have varying attitudes to and understanding of art, ranging from dismissive to informed and enthusiastic. A major part of your job, perhaps the most important part, is to support the development of positive attitudes to art in and beyond the school community. As you have been appointed art coordinator, it is reasonable to suppose that you yourself are an informed enthusiast. The work that you do with your children needs to reflect this and be a source of inspiration to teachers and pupils throughout the school.

In November 1996, the Teacher Training Agency (TTA) issued a consultation paper on 'Standards and a National Professional Qualification for Subject Leaders' (NPQSL) This delineates competencies for subject leaders, the term now used by the TTA, and it is proposed that subject leaders would be able to apply for a qualification in leadership of their subject area.

The draft national standards are in four main sections:

1   Core purpose for subject leaders
2   Key areas for development and assessment
(i)   teaching, learning and the curriculum
(ii)   monitoring, evaluating and improving
(iii)   people and relationships
(iv)   managing resources
(v)   accountability
3   Professional knowledge and understanding
4   Skills and abilities.   (TTA, 1996 p. 5)

The TTA document looks daunting but, when studied carefully, it becomes clear that these are manageable aspirations given the support of colleagues, headteacher and governors. Remember that all your colleagues in the primary school are likely to be subject leaders in at least one area. They need your support in these as much as you need theirs for art. You have the advantage of leading in a life-enhancing area, rich in possibilities for enjoyment. A major part of your job is to build up the confidence of colleagues. Make sure that you set manageable tasks and achievable goals for yourself and for them.

It is important to begin by being clear about your own position. Know your own strengths and shortcomings, and be honest about sharing your reflections with colleagues. Most people will respond readily to shared human confidence and be willing to confide in turn. A colleague who feels inadequate is quite likely to put up defences when confronted with an 'expert'. So having honestly identified where you stand, be sensitive in initiating discussion with colleagues, and always value their opinions and contributions.

Recent research into the readiness of primary schools to teach the NC in art (Clement, 1993) and *Art, A Review of Inspection Findings, 1993/4* (Ofsted, 1995) are of help to the subject leader in identifying areas where teachers are particularly lacking in confidence. (These reviews are updated regularly and issued by HMSO) In Clement's sample studied in 1993, one fifth of schools had no art Curriculum Coordinator and almost half had no policy or schemes of work for art. It is not the purpose here to speculate about why this situation was found but it might enable us to infer something about the status of art in a significant number of schools. When identifying starting points for helping colleagues and new members of staff, it is worth thoroughly exploring the NC document and ensuring shared understanding of its language, its aims and the strands which run throughout the key stages. Practical workshops involving all colleagues in activities that will enable them to succeed in developing skills at their own level need priority in time and funding, as do opportunities to engage with the work of other artists (see above for examples of such workshops).

Chapter 3

Working with the wider community

Attainment Target 2 holds most fears for many teachers who feel confident exploring tools and materials, but fear again this body of 'knowledge' which includes the experts and is foreign to the primary teacher. It is part of your role as subject leader to make the work of other artists and cultures accessible to your colleagues and to their pupils. You do not need a degree in the history of art to achieve this.

If finding time and a modest sum for workshops seems a daunting task, suggest a two-day course at one of the galleries offering guidance on engaging with art and design objects. You may succeed but if not, much can be achieved, again through workshops in school.

Part of your job is to ensure that your school is resourced with examples of the work of artists but your role should not end there. Colleagues need in varying degrees to be helped to engage with such work so that they can involve children in meaningful dialogue and appreciation.

A useful framework for initiating interaction with art objects is offered by Taylor (1992). He suggests four headings, Content, Form, Process and Mood. Under each heading is a series of key questions which will enable teachers to engage meaningfully with the art object and raise dialogue to a level above mere 'like it' or 'don't like it'. This dialogue can in turn be shared with children in modified form according to KS and language skills generally. Use of the framework, initially in staff workshops, will provide access to art works and is an alternative 'way in' or starting point for looking at other artists. It is less threatening and more accessible than having to begin by researching details and data concerning artists' lives and movements. Examples of some key questions under the four headings are:

1 **Content** What is the subject matter of the work, what is it about?
2 **Form**   How has the work been arranged?
3 **Process** How was the work made and what was it made with?
4 **Mood**   Does the work affect you, the viewer in any way? Does it capture a mood, feeling or emotion that you have already experienced?'

(Rod Taylor, *Visual Arts in Education*, 1992 p. 92)

The resources within the school will offer a range of opportunities to begin this process and initiate dialogue.

The Primary Art Pack (Clement and Page, 1994) offers a range of artefacts with suggestions for classroom related tasks. If your school has this resource, and many do, this could be used as a starting point for colleague interaction using Taylor's framework and key questions. The aim would be for staff members in small groups to be guided into responding to art objects in a non-threatening situation. Everyone's contribution is heard and none discounted. Colleagues who thought they 'knew nothing' about art and were previously tongue-tied when asked to offer comments about a work of art cannot fail, given access to this simple framework. The importance of teachers working together in this way cannot be over-emphasised.

Regular, honest reviews of progress and attitudes are important. Hopefully by this stage, as a staff, you will have made collective progress in practical skills and visual elements and in raising the level of discussion about, and interaction with, art objects. This will be evident also in classroom practice and dialogue with children.

An obvious progression will be to widen the range of resources to include the community outside the school, both locally and further afield. You need to make yourself aware of local talents and skills which can be brought to the school and shared with teachers and pupils. You also need to encourage colleagues to think positively about gallery visits. You need to be aware of such resources within the range of the school. These might include museums, LEA resources, libraries, higher education institutions, galleries etc. A list of sources and resources is included in Chapter 15, but you also need to be diligent in researching and investigating the wider resources in your own area.

Galleries and museums which have education departments encourage schools to use their collections. It is worth asking for samples of teaching packs, posters etc. explaining aspects of their collections which would relate to the National Curriculum requirements. It is also worth asking if they provide (free) practical workshops for children and staff.

An inservice gallery visit is invaluable. Many offer training days for teachers in organising gallery visits and ways of looking at art objects with primary children. Sometimes these are free, but there can be a fee involved. In the short-term you can organise your own day for staff in a local gallery and this can be regarded as a way of developing the staffroom starting-point using form, content, process and mood as a framework. No cost other than travelling expenses need be incurred. Colleagues can work in pairs or small groups, responding to a set number of art objects. These responses can be shared in a whole staff situation using inexpensive reproductions as references.

Colleagues should be encouraged to keep records of these responses in personal sketchbooks alongside their practical investigations and records of ideas. These form a further resource to be used with children, emphasising the value of the sketchbook to the process of artistic development at all levels.

It is clear that the National Curriculum demands that children should have some opportunities to visit galleries. This gives

Developing your role

However many strategies you devise for keeping costs to a minimum, some financial investment is necessary and a challenging part of your role is to convince the headteacher and governors that they want to make this investment and resource your subject appropriately.

The statutory requirements are clearly useful here, but you will not want to rely solely on threats and blandishments to convince others of the value of your subject and that it is deserving of proper funding. Your strengths lie in:

- your ability to motivate staff and develop their interest and enthusiasm, whatever their starting point;
- your success in initiating and developing colleagues' progress in investigating and making and in knowledge and understanding;
- your inventiveness so far in achieving the above within a low budget framework, resulting in visible benefits in attitudes, the environment of the school and, most importantly, in the pupils' experiences.

To further your claim for adequate funding to build upon progress so far, you need to present a clearly and tightly-budgeted plan for immediate and long-term investment. Practical workshop sessions with colleagues will have emphasised the need to train children in the care of tools and equipment but inevitably these need replacing when they wear out. Similarly, consumables need replenishing. If the fund-holders are convinced that your requests are based on carefully costed, genuine requirements they are more likely to cooperate.

Consider the following when submitting your claim for funding.
Have you consulted all staff about their needs?
Have you ensured that they prioritise in making requests?
Have you done a thorough stock check to avoid over-ordering?
Have you kept copies of everything?
Have you identified cost-effective quality suppliers for regular use?

Remember to ask for what is reasonable now but offer a long-term plan for expensive items prioritising affordable amounts for each year e.g. books, CD-ROM, slides, storage, kiln, etc.

them first-hand experience of original works and enhances their knowledge and understanding through direct experience, in addition to the secondary experience they receive through their teachers and through poster packs etc. As curriculum coordinator you should try to ensure that children have this experience at least once during the primary school years, if not once at each key stage. A visit to a local gallery should be within the school's means even if major art collections are too distant. A useful guide to museums and galleries is *The Art Directory* edited by Julian Homer 1993.

Reporting to heads, governors, parents and colleagues

The policy document is a crucial statement which ensures that governors, parents and colleagues have access to the school's aims and beliefs about the subject. It should be the product of whole staff collaboration and is a useful tool for reviewing and evaluating progress As such, it is a flexible document, subject to review and moderation itself as the school develops and changes.

Advice about the length and nature of policy documents has been varied and to some extent, therefore, bewildering. One side of A4 paper was the original recommendation in some educational texts, but it seems unlikely that, where a subject is valued across the curriculum, all that needs to be said could be fitted into such narrow confines.

It would be wrong to suggest that one model art policy could be written which would exactly meet the needs of every school. The content needs to be agreed in consultation with your colleagues so that teaching strengths are balanced and coordinated across the key stages and account is taken of local needs and resources as well as National Curriculum requirements. If all colleagues are involved and their contribution is valued, if their enjoyment and developing confidence in the subject is assured, the art policy should reflect the real place of art in the school and its importance in the school's overall plan for development.

The following headings provide the framework for the art policy of Sandiway County Primary School in Cheshire and are reproduced with the permission of the headteacher, Mrs. G. Thorley.

Art Policy — Sandiway County Primary School

1 Statement of principle
   This sets out the basic curriculum requirements in art, craft and design and includes a statement about why the school values art.

2 Aims or purpose
   This section outlines the opportunities, skills and abilities being developed. It acknowledges the importance of multicultural awareness and is an appropriate place to include reference to special provision required by some pupils and to state that children have equal access to the art curriculum.

3 Practice
   This section defines approaches and attitudes to art in and across the curriculum.

4 Organisation
   This outlines areas of responsibility and care for tools and materials.

5 Progress and continuity
   This is a statement about how consistency and continuity are safeguarded across the curriculum and across key stages.

6 Assessment
   This identifies the purposes of assessment, who it is for and how it is organised.

7 Recording and reporting
   This is factual information about how and where records are kept and the arrangements for reporting information to parents.

8 Resources
   Factual information including a list of basic materials, local galleries and museums, software, books, paintings, artefacts, resource centres and recommended reading.

The document concludes with a statement on Health and Safety and is signed and dated by the headteacher and chair of governors. The policy is subject to a biannual review.

(Sandiway C.P. School 1996. *My italics were used throughout*)

Developing performance indicators

A useful focus to aid review of progress can be found in *Art, A Review of Inspection Findings, 1993/94* (Ofsted, 1995) As stated earlier, this document is likely to be updated regularly so will provide an ongoing marker.

A policy document which has been agreed collaboratively should give an honest account of the school's beliefs and intentions. These should be evident in matching practice. A review of provision with particular reference to the general weaknesses identified by Ofsted (1995) would be a valuable staff exercise (see p. 5).

Rather than confront colleagues with a battery of shortcomings and weaknesses it is better to focus on manageable targets where there is clear room for development. *The Review of Findings* (Ofsted, 1995) is succinct and readable. Each member of staff could be invited to identify areas that they recognise as development points which could be applied to the school. The issues common to many schools and most likely to be raised by your colleagues are:

■ the need to map the breadth and balance of the art curriculum to ensure that skills, knowledge and understanding are being systematically developed and that National Curriculum Programmes of Study are being covered;

■ the need to approach the teaching of knowledge and understanding at Key Stages 1 and 2 carefully, avoiding mere copying of the work of artists;

■ the need to develop assessment in art;

■ the need to ensure that pupils of all ages have sufficient experience in three-dimensional work.

An honest review of the policy document, with a careful examination of the balance between reality and rhetoric will enable colleagues to identify where your school's priorities lie.

The need to map the breadth and balance of the curriculum should be a guiding factor in the development of a school scheme of work for art. As with the policy document, this needs to be a collaborative project which provides a framework for the development of the skills and visual elements across the school from under 5 to the beginning of Key Stage 3.

Many LEAs have produced guidelines for their schools. Addresses for enquiries about these are included in Chapter 15. The documents are intended to aid schools in the production of their schemes rather than to be prescriptive. In this respect they are a very useful resource.

Ways of enhancing knowledge and understanding have already been suggested. A pastiche of an artist's work or working in the style of another artist can be useful exercises in their place, but as OFSTED (1995) point out, more is needed. The activities designed to lead teachers and children into the work of other artists provide a valuable basis here and this includes three-dimensional as well as two-dimensional work.

Whatever you and your colleagues decide to focus on, first make sure that progress is achievable in the time stated and that progress is real, not token.

The vital issue of assessment is addressed in Part 4 but general points can be re-affirmed here. Art has not received the detailed guidance in assessment that some subject areas have 'enjoyed'. The general End of Key Stage Descriptors provide the summative assessment offered by the National Curriculum.

It is recommended, though not required, that portfolios are kept. Beyond that the schools must make their own decisions and provision for formative assessment. It is worth re-stating that in art as in other subject areas, we assess children's work to:
- monitor their progress and inform our plans for progress;
- confirm that we practise what we say in our statements of beliefs and that we are monitoring this;
- provide information for others about the children's progress;
- include the children in the process of assessment and personal development.

In your subject, you are responsible for ensuring that rigorous intellectual standards are being applied across the school, but also that the joy and satisfaction of creative achievement is assured for every child.

Part two   What art coordinators
             need to know

Chapter 4   Subject knowledge

Like every art coordinator, you will bring a variety of experience, knowledge and some warmth towards the teaching of art to your task of managing the art curriculum in your school. Your colleagues will think of you as the school's 'art expert' and will look to you for advice about the **content of what they should teach in art**. Because children ideally have to be taught to use a wide range of materials, processes and resources in order to make art, your colleagues will also seek a lot of help and advice about **how they should teach art**.

You don't have to be an expert in all aspects of art teaching to be an effective team leader, although you do need to be confident enough in you own teaching of art to be able to lead by example in teaching some aspects of art and design.

Much of the support you will provide to colleagues can come from other sources, for example, through good documentation of the school's work in art, through providing access to good publications about teaching art and, most importantly, by your identifying and building upon the strengths and interests of your colleagues in teaching both art and other subjects.

In teaching art well, you will use many teaching strategies that are common to the teaching of all subjects, such as the skills of questioning, of generating discourse, of focusing enquiry and investigation, of matching resources to tasks. For example, the teacher's skill in using questioning to focus children's looking is much more important to the teaching of drawing from observation than the teacher's own skills in making a drawing!

There are significant overlaps between the way that children make art and the ways that they make and use language, or undertake investigation and enquiry in their work in science: between how they make art and how they make sense of their experiences through the use of other subject disciplines.

In your work as art coordinator, you will need to strike a nice balance between being the 'art expert' and being the good facilitator who can help colleagues to see how they can bring their own experiences and skills in teaching to support the way in which they teach art to children with their own class groups.

The aims for art education in the National Curriculum

It is sensible to begin by considering what are the principle aims for teaching art in Key Stages 1 and 2 and how these correspond to the things that you think are important to you and your colleagues in teaching art in your school.

Like all subjects, the teaching of art has its own pattern of aims and intentions that have been established over many years of practice in schools and which have been confirmed and clarified through the establishment of Attainment Targets and Programmes of Study for the subject, in the shaping of the National Curriculum in art.

In the final report from the art working party *Art for Ages 5–14*, the aims for art education in the National Curriculum were identified as follows:

- Developing a sense of enjoyment, self-esteem and achievement in making art
- Developing skills in handling materials and processes in art
- Developing the ability to draw from observation
- Developing the ability to design and make artefacts
- Developing visual skills that can be used across the curriculum
- Developing the powers of imagination, originality and personal expression
- Developing skills in using and handling the visual elements of art (colour, line, tone, pattern, texture, shape, form and space)

- Developing visual literacy: the ability to read and understand images
- Developing aesthetic sensibility: the ability to make informed judgments about art
- Developing the ability to communicate ideas and feelings about the work of artists and designers   (DfE, 1992)

How do you rate these aims in your own practice in teaching art? Which aims do you consider to be very important? Which of these aims are less important to you in teaching art to children in a primary school?

Obviously, some of these aims, like *Developing visual literacy, the ability to read and understand images* are more likely to be important to teachers working with older pupils in Key Stage 3.

Some of these aims, like *Teaching visual skills that can be used across the curriculum*, are more likely to be important to you in your work with children in primary schools.

What are your aims?

You might find it helpful to work your way through this list of aims, consider your own intentions in teaching art to children over the years and then place these aims in your own personal rank order! Like the vast majority of primary school teachers you will almost certainly place *Developing a sense of enjoyment, self-esteem and achievement in making art* at the top of your list. But where do the rest of these aims come? What does this tell you about your own intentions in teaching art?

What do your colleagues in school think about these aims? Do your colleagues in school share your aims and intentions? You might find it very revealing to ask them to rate these aims in relation to their own teaching and thinking about art and to see how much consensus there might be in your own school as to what we think we are doing in teaching art to children!

Useful references

DfE (1992) *Art for Ages 5 to 14*, London: HMSO.

Teaching skills and processes

In order to match the aims for the National Curriculum in art, you have to teach children a range of skills and processes, give them an understanding of art and design concepts and some knowledge about the work of artists and designers.

Listed below are those competencies that children have to be taught in Key Stages 1 and 2 to in order to match National Curriculum requirements.

You will find it useful to check through these and to identify which of these you think you are dealing with at varying degrees of effectiveness in your own teaching and which you need to know more about in order to give appropriate leadership to your colleagues.

Against each competency, indicate on the following scale your level of confidence in dealing with this area.
1 I do this very well
2 I am competent
3 I need to improve

National Curriculum requirements

1	Drawing and painting from observation of made/ natural forms	1	2	3
2	Drawing and painting from memory/imagination	1	2	3
3	Investigating and using a range of resources as stimulus for work	1	2	3
4	Developing and recording ideas through sketch books	1	2	3
5	Two dimensional design (e.g. print making/textiles)	1	2	3
6	Three dimensional design (e.g. modelling/clay work)	1	2	3
7	Using the work of artists and designers as reference and stimulus material for making images and artefacts	1	2	3
8	Knowledge of the work of artists/craftworkers and designers	1	2	3
9	Pupils reviewing and evaluating their own work and that of other artists and designers	1	2	3

In the light of this review identify three key priorities for your own inservice training/reading.

1

2

3

You can also use this same list of competencies to check the state of play in teaching art across the different year groups in your own school and this possibility is discussed in more detail in Part 3.

Attainment targets and key strands

As a subject coordinator, you will already be familiar with, and confident in using and teaching, many of the Programmes of Study for art.

In working with colleagues and in helping them to understand and use the art framework in their own teaching, you will find it useful to refer to the following description which illustrates the relationship between the *two Attainment Targets* and the *six Key Strands* which form the basis for constructing the *Programmes of Study in Art.* Alongside each Key Strand there is a simplified description of what children have to be taught within that strand.

The six key strands	
In Attainment Target 1 Investigating and Making	
Investigating	
a **Record responses, including observations of the natural and made environment**	Making drawings and studies of familiar natural and made forms and of ideas and experiences from memory and imagination in order to develop the skills of recording ideas and observations.
b **Gather resources and materials, using them to stimulate and develop ideas**	Providing pupils with a rich range of starting points and resources for making work and teaching them the investigative skills to explore, sort and develop ideas through visual research including using sketch books.
Making	
c **Explore and use two and three dimensional media, working on a variety of scales**	Developing skills in handling and using a range of materials and processes in drawing and painting and in designing and making work in printmaking, textiles and in three dimensional media. Learning to understand and use the visual elements of colour, line, tone, texture, shape, form and space in making work in art.
d **Review and modify their work as it progresses**	Talking and writing about what they have made in art, how they have made it, what they think and feel about the work they have made and how it might be modified and improved in making future work.

In Attainment Target 2 Knowledge and Understanding	
Knowledge	
e **Develop understanding of the work of artists, craftspeople and designers, and applying knowledge to their own work**	Learning about the way that other artists have made work, how they have used the visual elements of art and how they can use this knowledge in making their own work.
	Learning about the different ideas and feelings that artists have explored in making their work and exploring similar ideas in making their own work.
f **Respond to and evaluate different art, craft and design, including their own and other's work**	Describing, comparing and contrasting work made by artists using different methods and media and working in different times and cultures.
	Developing the vocabulary to express ideas and opinions about their own work and work made by other artists.

When working with your colleagues you may find it helpful to look at some recent practice in your own school to identify how these six strands of working in art relate to each other, overlap, and may be used in different ways as the basis for planning work in art with children.

This can easily be done by looking at a recent art project and making diagrams of how the different strands come into play and overlap as the work progresses through its various stages.

In the two examples (left), the strands occur in very different sequences —

b / a / e / c / c / d / f **and** e / f / a / b / f / c / f

One project begins in work related to AT1 and the other in work centred on AT2.

Through reviewing what you and your colleagues are teaching in art in this way, you can give them a better understanding of how the Programmes of Study can be used flexibly to deliver the Attainment Target requirements. It is also a useful way to check the balance of use across the Key Strands of teaching in art, across a year's programme of work.

The examples shown in Figures 4.1, 4.2, 4.3, 4.4 and 4.5, based on Degas' dancers, are of illustrations of children's work from Key Stage 1, Year 2. You should be able to demonstrate the working relationship between the six Key Strands in your own school through the way in which you display and explain children's work. The didactic use of display is developed further in Part 4 of this book.

An example of how different strands relate as work progresses

Year 2 project
Plants

(b) collecting and sorting plants ⟶
(a) making drawings of natural forms ⟶
(e) looking at other artist's use of colour ⟶
(c) making colour studies from plants ⟶
(c) making paintings ⟶
(d) reflecting upon the work ⟶
(f) comparing their own use of colour with that of other artists

Year 5 project
Interiors

(e) comparing paintings of interiors by three different artists ⟶
(f) making studies to explain differences ⟶
(a) making drawings of rooms at home ⟶
(b) comparing and considering how rooms could be improved ⟶
(f) evaluating progress ⟶
(c) making models in paper or clay of an ideal room ⟶
(f) comparing models with original starting points

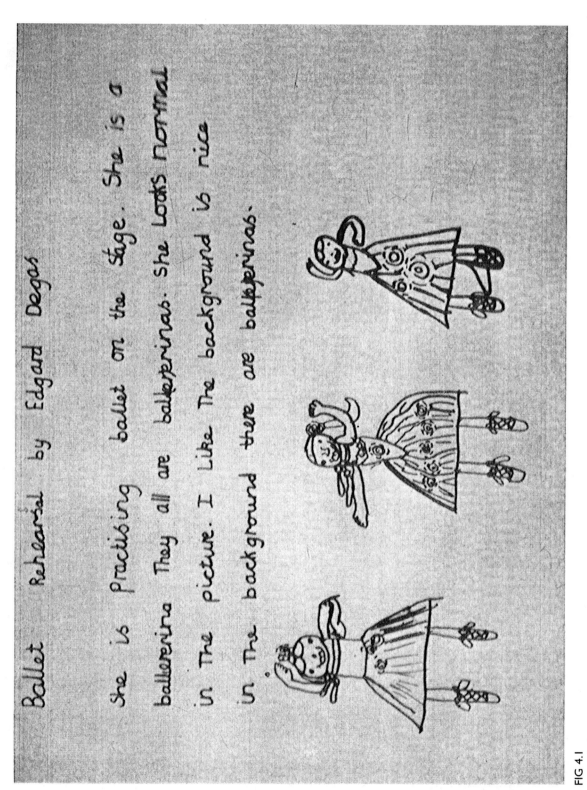

Ballet Rehearsal by Edgard Degas

She is Practising ballet on the Stage. She is a ballerina They all are ballerinas. She Looks normal in The picture. I Like The background is nice in The background there are ballerinas.

FIG 4.1
Ballet Rehearsal — illustrated description of painting by Degas: fibre tip pen

FIG 4.2
Two Dancers — 'Keyhole' studies
of dancers from paintings by Degas:
pencil

FIG 4.3
Study of a dancer: pastel and crayon

FIG 4.4
Dancer — study of a child dancing for the class: pencil

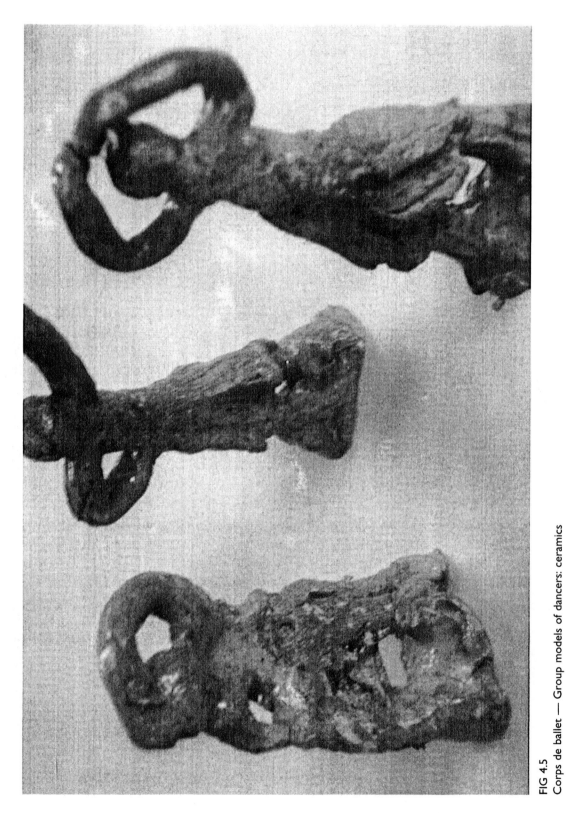

FIG 4.5
Corps de ballet — Group models of dancers: ceramics

The illustrations of children's work at Key Stage 2 (Yr6) based on designs by William Morris, are shown in Figures 4.6, 4.7, 4.8, 4.9, 4.10, 4.11.

Understanding the relationship between AT1 and AT2

The examples provided on pp. 40–52 should help to illustrate how the two Attainment Targets for art can be used flexibly to interact with each other and to complement and build upon their respective Programmes of Study.

This should be a useful reminder that the two Attainment Targets should always be interactive although they are concerned respectively with teaching children **how to make art** and with helping children **to understand art**. These practical and critical aspects of teaching art are complementary and essential to each other in the successful teaching of the subject.

We can see this most clearly in the development of art in our own culture and the way that artists, craftworkers and designers have progressively developed their own individual styles through the influence of the work of other artists.

This was most simply expressed by the painter, Georges Braque in his statement

 All art springs from nature and from art.

Our desire to make art springs from our experiences in the world: we learn how to make art by looking at the way it has been made by other artists.

You can help colleagues who are reluctant or who have difficulty in recognising this link between making and understanding in art by drawing a parallel between the way that they teach children the use of language, sharing with their pupils the work of other writers, story-tellers and poets to give them a better understanding of the possibilities of language.

FIG 4.6
Victorian printing block

FIG 4.7
Cushion with Williams Morris design

FIG 4.8
Keyhole studies from William Morris fabrics: pencil

FIG 4.9
Design for wallpaper: fibre tip pen

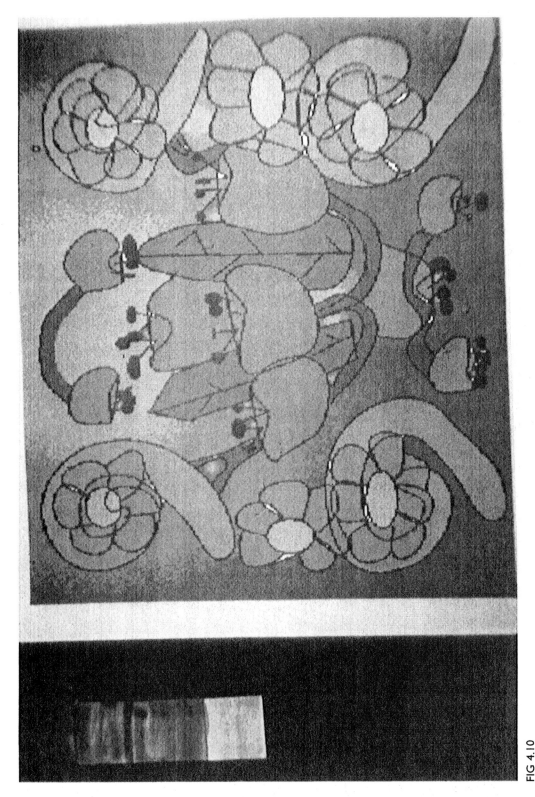

FIG 4.10
Unit design for wallpaper: computer-aided drawing

FIG 4.11
Model of Victorian room: mixed media

Through exploring different forms and vocabulary you can expand the children's ability to write about their experiences. By giving the children the experience of many writers you widen their understanding and appreciation of language.

In teaching art we can use other artists' work to give children a better understanding of the possibilities of image making. They can apply their own knowledge of the way that other artists make work to their own making. Children can also learn a great deal about the way that ideas are expressed in art through looking at the many ways that artists have communicated ideas and feelings through making art in different times.

When the key components of the National Curriculum in art are set out as below it is possible to see how they can interact and how activity in making art can begin and can be rooted in any of these key elements and can take different kinds of routes through these components, depending upon the nature of the project (Figure 4.12).

FIG 4.12
Key components of the National Curriculum for art

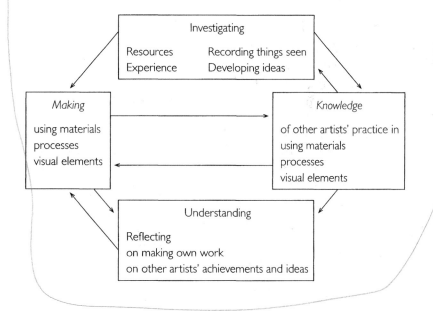

Chapter 5   Understanding how children progress in making art

You will need to able to give your colleagues detailed guidance and support as to what kind of work it is most suitable to undertake with children at different stages in their primary schooling. To do this you do need to have some grasp of the way that children's making of images is matched to their changing perceptions of the world as they progress through your school.

This aspect of children's work in art is dealt with in some detail in Chapter 13, as understanding progression in children's image making is a crucial element in monitoring and recording children's achievements in art. It is also linked to the following section on **the functions of drawing** because such progression is most immediately evident in the way that children's drawings develop and change between the ages of four and eleven.

It is very obvious that the kinds of drawing that children make in Nursery and Reception classes are very different from those made by children in Years 5 and 6, especially when we look at drawings made by children at different ages from common starting points. The five-year-old records her own appearance or describes her house for very different reasons and using different systems to the eleven-year-old child (Figures 5.1, 5.2, 5.3, 5.4).

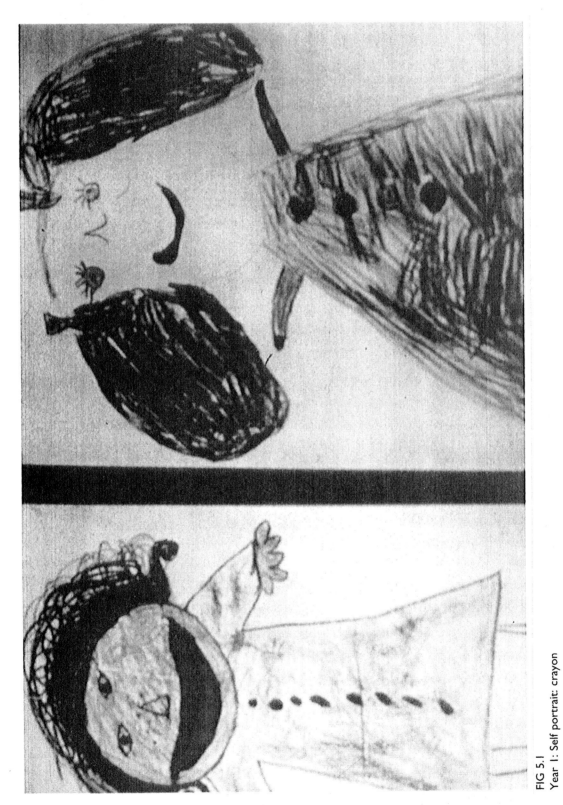

FIG 5.1
Year 1: Self portrait: crayon

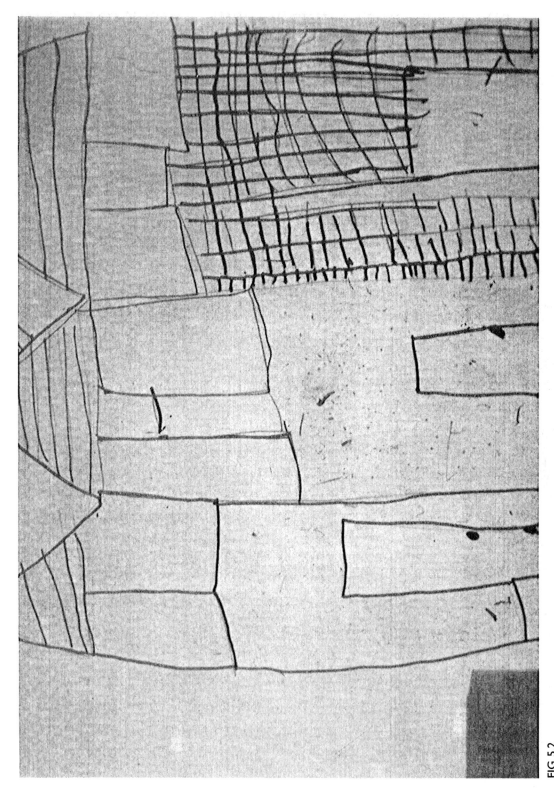

FIG 5.2
My house, Yr 1: pencil

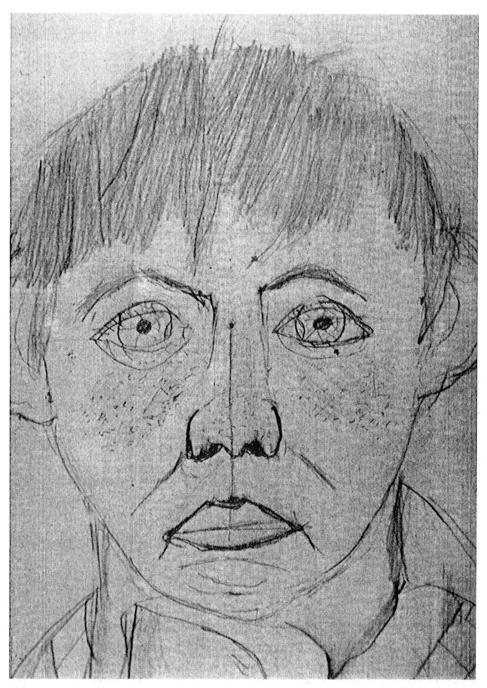

FIG 5.3
Self portrait, Yr 6: pencil

FIG 5.4
My house, Yr 6: fibre tip pens

How children progress in making images

The following summary attempts to descibe the progression that children make from their first scribbles and symbols in drawing and painting to their making of descriptive, comparative and analytical drawings in Years 5 and 6.

1   Children's first drawings and paintings grow out of their scribblings with crayons and pencils and their 'playing' with paint. They begin by identifying or **'naming'** the shapes and patterns they make in this play with materials. They **identify** things or experiences they associate with the shapes that they make. These circles, shapes, squiggles and lines come to **stand for** the people they know and the familiar things they enjoy.

2   As they develop more motor control they begin to use these **symbols** more specifically to **explain** (not to describe) experiences that are important to them.

3   Most children by the age of five can use symbolic drawings and paintings to **explain** and **tell stories** about their experiences. At this stage they can use drawings to recount their experience more confidently than they can use language because they have access to a very flexible visual language of visual symbols. They draw and paint what they **know**, not what they **see**. It doesn't concern them that their images do not describe the things they see! They will draw things they have experienced and things they have seen confidently from **memory**.

4   Between the ages of 5 and 7, children's use of formal language improves significantly. They acquire the skills to write and talk more confidently about their experiences. Consequently, their need to use drawings to communicate their ideas and experiences begins to decline. They begin to recognise that drawings and paintings have **public meaning** as much as **private satisfaction** and that there are recognised conventions for the way that we **describe and represent our ideas** through drawings. They will as happily make story-telling drawings from **memory** as simple descriptive drawing from **direct observation**.

5   In the transition from Key Stage 1 to Key Stage 2, children increasingly begin to introduce **descriptive** elements into their drawings and paintings. They want and need to **explain what things look like** in their work in art. They

become more concerned with **appearance and detail**. At this transitional stage they will use intriguing combinations of symbolic representation and real description in their work.

6   During their work in Key Stage 2, children will develop confidence and skills in using their drawings and paintings to make **careful descriptions** of familiar things within the environment and can make increasingly subtle **comparisons** between similar forms. They begin to lose confidence in their powers to draw from recall because they no longer give value to the symbolic systems of drawing that allow younger children to recall complex experiences.

7   As their skills develop in handling materials and in understanding and using such visual elements as line, tone, colour and texture, they will begin to use drawing and painting media more **selectively** to focus upon particular visual qualities within their visual environment. Their drawing will become more **analytical** and concerned as much with recording **formal visual qualities** as with descriptive appearance.

It will be useful for you to check this description of progress and change in children's image making against your own and your colleagues' experience of teaching children at different stages in the primary school.

Useful references

Rhoda Kellogg (1969) *Analysing Children's Art* (Mayfield Publishing Company ISBN 0 874 196 8)

Margaret Morgan (1988) *Art 4–11* (Oxford: Blackwell ISBN 0 631 90166 3)

Robert Clement and Shirley Page 1992 *Principles and Practice in Art* (London: Oliver and Boyd ISBN 0 050 05082 6)

The drawings and paintings in Figures 5.5, 5.6, 5.7, 5.8, 5.9, showing a sequence of drawings of a seated figure, illustrate this development and change through the way that children make drawings and paintings in response to a very familiar starting point for work.

FIG 5.5
Reception: Seated figure from observation

FIG 5.6
Yr 1: Seated figure from
observation

In your school, you will find it very helful to put together
similar collections of children's work from different year
groups and from a common starting point to use in discussion
with your colleagues about the way that children's work in art
develops from Reception to Year 6.

The centrality and function of drawing

Drawing is the **essential core activity** to all our work
in art with children in schools. It should be evident from
the previous section that understanding and managing the

FIG 5.7
Yr 2: Seated figure from
observation

development of children's image making through their work
in drawing is crucial towards establishing and supporting
children's progress in making art.

In your work in teaching, you will almost certainly have
worked with colleagues who have found it difficult to teach
drawing to their own classes because of their own perceived
lack of skills in making drawings themselves.

❛ *I don't teach drawing because I can't draw*

is a common complaint and cry for help from primary school
teachers!

FIG 5.8
Yr 3: Seated figure from
observation

Giving your colleagues the support, understanding and
confidence to take the teaching of drawing seriously with their
own classes may well be an important hurdle for you to
overcome in your work as a coordinator in your school.

Drawing in the National Curriculum

The important place that drawing has in art in the National
Curriculum is emphasised through its dominance in the Key
Strand of Investigating in Attainment Target 1.

FIG 5.9
Yr 4: Seated figure from observation

Children should be taught:

> to make drawings and studies of familiar natural and manmade forms, and of ideas and experiences from memory and imagination, in order to develop the skills of recording ideas and observations;

> the investigative skills to explore, sort and develop ideas through visual research including using sketchbooks.

Different kinds of drawing

We ask and teach children to make different kinds of drawing for different purposes.

As has already been discussed earlier in this chapter, it is evident that children make and use drawings in different kinds of ways as they progress through your school and that their drawings are made and used for different purposes as they progress from one stage of understanding to another.

In association with looking at the way that children's work progresses and changes from year to year it would be helpful to you and your colleagues to collect examples of these different kinds of drawings so that you can share together, and, through discussion about them, become more familiar with and confident about understanding the different purposes for which drawings are made. You might well include examples of these for guidance within your art policy documents.

Put together a collection of work from different year groups yourself, using the following descriptions to help you identify drawings made for different kinds of purposes. Encourage indvidual staff to do this within their own class group so that they can review at the end of a term or year what balance of different kinds of drawings they have undertaken with their own class.

Story-telling or narrative drawings
are the natural consequence of the way that young children in Key Stage 1 use drawings to recall and respond to their early experiences. They will make drawings to recall things, occasions or events that are important to them, for example, a

favourite toy, playing with friends, a birthday party. They will make drawings that tell stories and remind them about things they have done or would like to experience. All narrative drawings are made from recall or memory of the event. They are imaginative reconstructions of the child's experience.

Explaining drawings

are made by children as they develop in their confidence in using symbols to explain some of the things that they see and experience. In these drawings they use symbols to tell us what they know about things they see as much as to describe what they see. They are made from combinations of recall and observation. For example, a drawing of the family outing by car will be organised so that we can see all members of the family inside the car and will inlcude different view points of the car in the same drawing to explain everything the child knows! In these drawings and in order to 'explain' more clearly, they will begin to introduce descriptive elements.

Descriptive or observational drawings

are made to record and describe the appearance of everyday natural, manmade and environmental forms. In making these drawings, children become increasingly concerned to **represent** what they see through detailed description of the forms they are studying. They can begin in Key Stage 1 as 'careful looking drawings' where children are asked to explain what simple and familiar things look like.

Comparative drawings

are a natural extension of descriptive drawings and where children make studies of similar but different forms to distinguish between them and to encourage them to look closely and to make more subtle distinctions in the use of such visual elements as line, tone, pattern and form in making the drawings.

Analytical drawings

are made through focusing upon particular aspects of the things they see and through selecting and making studies of such visual elements as pattern, texture and structure in natural and manmade forms in the environment.

Exploratory and investigative drawings
are made to collect information and to explore ideas for making work. In Key Stage 2, these play an important part in the work that children undertake in their sketchbooks.

A balance of drawings

It is important to try to maintain a balance in the use of different kinds of drawings made by children in Key Stages 1 and 2, through setting them different kinds of drawing tasks and also by taking account of what kinds of drawings they make in support of other curriculum work.

In Key Stage 1, the predominant methods of drawing used will tend to be:
    Story-telling
    Explanatory
    Descriptive (or 'Careful Looking' drawings)
    Comparative

Although story-telling and explanatory drawings will dominate, it is important to encourage teachers working in Key Stage 1 to introduce and use descriptive or careful looking drawing throughout the Key Stage so that the children are developing the skills of observation alongside their more intuitive and spontaneous use of drawing to recount and recall experiences.

In Key Stage 2, the predominant methods of drawing used will tend to be:
    Descriptive
    Comparative
    Analytical
    Investigative

Many of the drawings that children undertake in Key Stage 2 will be made in association with their work in science, technology, history and geography and where they will use their developing powers of observation and analysis to record and investigate natural forms and phenonema along with made forms and environments.

Drawing to make copies

As curriculum leader for art, you will also need to monitor and occasionally issue 'health warnings' about the tendency by some teachers to allow too much use by children of drawing to make copies from secondary sources. This occurs most frequently in cross-curricular work and where it is occasionally necessary for children to make a copy of an illustration from a textbook to illustrate or extend their writing and research.

This can become a problem if and when making 'copies' becomes too dominant an activity in a particular class or year group and when teachers mistakenly think that making copies from books, illustrations or photographs is a justifiable drawing activity in its own right! Children's abilities in drawing are not extended through making copies — indeed, too much reliance or dependence upon copying will eventually diminish the child's ability and confidence to make a drawing.

You can obviously help colleagues to avoid this copying dependency trap by giving them good examples of ways in which they can use real experiences and richer resources to match the requirements of the topic being studied, so that when children are 'illustrating' their topic work they are undertaking drawing tasks that have some value in their own right.

For example, when illustrating a topic on transport, children will be more usefully employed in making one or two drawings from three dimensional toys or models of cars or making drawings of staff cars in the car park, than copying pictures of cars from books. Similarly, making studies from reproductions of paintings or miniatures by Tudor artists of the Tudor royal families is far more supportive to their developing skills in art than copying pictures of the kings and queens in topic books.

Methodologies for teaching drawing

The methodologies for teaching children how to draw are dealt with in more detail in the following sections on the teaching strategies and the resources you use in teaching children how to make art.

It is sufficient here to reinforce that link between the different kinds of drawings that children make and the way that the drawing task is framed for them and placed in context through that combination of talk, discussion and observation used and generated by the teacher.

It is a useful exercise for you and your colleagues to take any of the familiar starting points for drawing you use in your work with children and consider what different directions the response may take, depending upon the questions you ask the children in order to encourage them to think about and respond to the task.

For example, what kind of work and response might follow upon your giving the children the familiar task of making a portrait drawing when setting the task in different kinds of contexts.

The portrait   After looking at pictures of babies, draw what you think you looked like as a baby.

Draw from memory
(a) what you think you look like now;
(b) what you would like to look like now.

After looking at photographs of your family, draw what you think you will look like when you are grown up.

Using a mirror make a drawing of yourself from observation.

Work with a friend and using a mirror make studies to compare different parts of your face with your friend's face — how are your eyes, ears, mouths, noses etc., different from each other?

Look at reproductions of self portrait drawings by two different artists. Compare their drawing methods. Make a drawing of yourself using using a similar method of drawing.

Suggestion

Referring to the particular context for portrait drawing can you make a similar list of the different kinds of drawing activities that might flow from other familiar starting points? Can you then identify which drawing tasks would be most appropriate to children in Key Stage 1 or Key Stage 2?

Sketchbooks

Although the use of sketchbooks does not 'officially' feature as part of the National Curriculum in art in Key Stage 1 — and appears only in the Programmes of Study for Key Stage 2, many schools have introduced their use as early as Year 1 in the belief that it is valuable for young children to become accustomed to the habit of using sketchbooks both to practise their drawing and to record ideas and observations about the art they make and see.

They also have added value to the teacher in that it is much easier to refer to the range of work that individual children have done and to monitor their progress, when much of it is encompassed within one sketchbook that is easy to store and that can be passed from teacher to teacher as the the children progress through the school. The use of sketchbooks to monitor to children's work is discussed further on p. 161.

The traditional term 'sketchbook' can be misleading. A good sketchbook should be a combination of notebook and artist's diary and provide evidence of what references and resources children have used to show how their ideas have developed, in addition to the more traditional sketchbook drawings. A sketchbook might include the following:

- drawings;
- photocopies of drawings and paintings made by the children;
- photographs;
- reproductions of works of art;
- comments and notes about things they have made;
- sketches and working drawings for things they want to make;
- notes on technical processes;
- personal comments about and descriptions of things they have made;
- writing about other artist's work they have seen.

Useful references

Gillian Robinson (1995) *Sketch-books: Explore and Store* (London: Hodder and Stoughton, ISBN 0 340 61117 0)
Dawn and Fred Sidgwick (1993) *Drawing to Learn* (London: Hodder and Stoughton ISBN 0 340 57341 4)
Maureen Cox (1990) *Children's Drawings* (Penguin ISBN 0 14 013910 9)

Critical studies

That area of work in art that we have come to call Critical Studies now dominates Attainment Target 2, Knowledge and Understanding in the National Curriculum in art.

The Programmes of Study for AT2 summarise what children have to be taught in association with this Attainment Target.

Knowledge	Learning about the way that other artists have made work, how they have used the visual elements of art and how they can use this knowledge in making their own work.
	Learning about the different ideas and feelings that artists have explored in making their work and exploring similar ideas in making their own work.
Understanding	Describing, comparing and contrasting work made by artists using different methods and media and working in different times and cultures.
	Developing the vocabulary to express ideas and opinions about their own work and work made by other artists.

The National Curriculum statements also emphasise that, wherever possible, Attainment Targets 1 and 2 should be taught in harness so that the critical aspects of children's work in art are always closely linked to their practical Investigating and Making. It is also emphasised that by artists we mean artists, craftworkers and designers and that children should be taught about achievement in art across a wide range of disciplines in art, craft and design.

For many of your colleagues, working effectively with Attainment Target 2 presents a combination of stimulus, challenge and demand. For them, teaching children about art, as well as how to make it, is a new and demanding area of work. While many teachers have welcomed the wider range of reference for making work in art that Critical Studies demands, others have been concerned about their own lack of knowledge about art and artists and how this will affect their teaching.

You can help your colleagues to see the logic in using other artists' work as stimulus for teaching children to make their own work by making a parallel between the way we teach art and the way that, in teaching language, pp. 46 and 53, we use other writers' and story-tellers' work as stimulus and to give children an understanding of the possibilities of language. In teaching language we attempt to teach children both to use the structure and vocabulary of language as well as how to use language to explore a range of ideas and feelings.

In art, in using critical studies methods, you can use other artists' work to teach children how to make work as, for example, in using a range of work by different painters to teach children how to understand and use colour. You can also use the study of other artists' work to help children to understand how they can express their own ideas and feelings in different kinds of ways through making their own work in art.

Limits and constraints

Although work in critical studies has generated exciting developments in many schools, in others, the work is narrow and lacking in ambition because of a variety of limits and constraints. These constraints may be linked to **poor resourcing for the work or because teachers are using critical studies within a narrow frame of reference**. In some schools, children are given access only to a narrow range of artists — usually the Impressionist and Post-Impressionist painters (where Monet, Van Gogh and Matisse reign supreme!) and the work the children make from their study of other artists' work is limited to simple pastiche.

While there is value in using pastiche (or borrowing) with younger pupils and the choice of artists we use is often determined by affordable texts, as coordinator you will need to review how critical studies methods and resources are being used in your school and provide a framework within which this work can best develop and progress.

How many different kinds of ways is art being used in your school? Is there evidence of developmental work in critical studies from Key Stage 1 to Key Stage 2?

A range of methodologies

The checklist that follows may be a useful starting point from which you will be able to review how this essential element of teaching art is being managed and developed in your school.

Pastiche (borrowing)	Sharing with the teacher, observing and talking about works by artists that explore subject matter and ideas that relate to the children's own experiences and then making their own versions of the work in drawing, painting or modelling
Working directly from	Making studies directly from observation of a work to learn more about the way it was made (for example, how colour is used and paint applied) or how the subject matter and ideas have been presented
Working in the style of	Studying the way an artist has made a work and then using similar methods to make their own work based on similar subject matter (for example making a painting of their own bedroom after viewing Van Gogh's painting of his room at Arles)
Simulation	Recreating in the classroom the subject matter of a familiar painting (for example, by dressing up one pupil like the character in a portrait painting) and after comparison of the subject matter with the way that the artist has interpreted the figure and made the work, make work from the figure themselves
Studying artists' methods	Making studies from sections or details of works by different artists to compare different methods of using materials and processes (for example, the different ways that line can be used in making a drawing) and using these methods in making their own work
Analysing visual elements	Comparing and contrasting the different ways that artists use colour, line, tone, texture, shape, form and space in making work through making studies from a range of work
Change of media/scale	Studying work in one media and translating it into another through using different materials or working on a different scale (for example, reconstructing a landscape painting three dimensionally as a diorama or by making a clay model of painting of a group of figures)
Comparing and contrasting	Making practical comparative studies to explain the differences between the way that two different artists have made very different work from the same kind of starting point
Making work in context	Studying, analysing and reconstructing work made in a different time or culture (for example, a Medieval icon, Tudor miniature or Aboriginal time line painting) to understand better the context within which the work was made
Influences and developments	Making studies from the work of artists and designers to identify how the work of one artist influences another and how artists learn from, build upon and develop their own ideas through the influence and work of others

Resources and reference materials for work in critical studies

Resourcing work in critical studies will be a major concern for you in your school as the range and quality of resources you have available, both within the school and within the environment of your community, will have a significant bearing upon the quality of exerience you can provide for the children in your school about the work of artists, craftworkers and designers.

Although you can give children a good start to their work in learning about the work of other artists through using such secondary source material as books, posters and postcards, you will need to seek further and more immediate experience of artists and the work they make in order to give the children a real sense of what artists can achieve. Children (and teachers) who have witnessed artists at work and who have had opportunities to see the work of artists and designers at first hand at exhibitions in museums, galleries and studios will have a much richer understanding of the artist's work.

Resources in the school

Resources in the school
(including those available from libraries, loan collections etc.)
Children's books with good illustrations by artists
Artefacts made by craftworkers e.g.:
    pots
    woven fabrics
    printed fabrics
Artefacts, including facsimiles of work from other cultures
Collections of familiar designed forms e.g.:
    tea pots
    hats
    toys etc.
Good quality photographs
Original paintings, drawings or prints

Resources in the locality and environment
Buildings
Public sculpture
Murals

Suggestion

Review with your colleagues which of the following references and resources you have access to for your teaching of critical studies and use this review to forward plan ways in which you can extend and use further the range of evidence of the work of artists available to children in your school.

Craft shops and workshops
Artists' studios

Exhibitions at   arts centres
                   galleries
                   museums
                   schools of art
                   public venues

Artists   working in your community
                   parents
                   students at local colleges
                   colleagues teaching in local secondary schools
                   and colleges

Reference materials

Postcards, posters or books for work in art, history and religious education referring to work by artists and designers from the following times, or cultures:

Egyptian	Greek	Roman
Chinese	Japanese	African
Indian	Islamic	North American
South American	Viking	Anglo Saxon
Celtic	Tudor	Victorian

Books, posters and postcards, videos or slides refererring to work from the following times and periods:

Renaissance	Reformation	19th century genre paintings
Pre-Raphaelites	Impressionism	Post-Impressionism
Cubism	Surrealism	20th century Figurative
Abstraction	Contemporary (work by living artists)	

Which of the following designers and craftsworkers are represented in your collections of reference material?

Architects   Potters   Fabric designers   Print makers

Developing and using a critical vocabulary

Children can only come to make judgments, to express ideas and opinions about their own work and that of other artists and designers if they have the critical vocabulary to do this.

Obviously enough, this vocabulary will emerge when and where they have frequent opportunities to share their views and perceptions about their own and other artists' work, both with their teachers and with each other. This use of reviewing and discussion about work is developed further (see pp. 148–50) as review and self-evaluation play an important part in the monitoring and appraisal of children's progress in making and understanding art.

Wherever possible, opportunities for discussion and review should be built into the teaching and practice of making art. Sometimes this will flow naturally enough through the common sharing and discussion about progress and achievement in the work that takes place both as a structured class activity and through negotiation and discussion with individual children.

You will need to ensure that such practice is an accepted part of teaching art in your school and to encourage your colleagues to give children regular opportunities to talk and write about their work in art, to describe how they make it and to describe and comment upon other artists' work.

You may need to suggest simple frameworks for such discussion and review. With younger children it may be sufficient to ask them such simple questions as:

> *How do you think this work was made?*
> *What do you think this work is about — what story does it tell?*

With older children you can use such frameworks as those proposed by Rod Taylor in his writing about critical studies in *Education in Art* and, where he suggests that by encouraging children to review work under the following headings, this should lead to a better understanding of the significance of the work.

Process How is the work made?
What materials and processes have been used?
How have they been used?

Content What is the work about?
What story does it tell?
What ideas or feelings does it express?

Form How has the artist used the visual elements of colour, line, tone, texture, form and space in making this work?

Mood How does this painting make you feel?
What mood does it convey?

Useful references

Rod Taylor (1986) *Educating for Art* (London: Longman ISBN 0 582 36152 4)

Robert Clement and Shirley Page (1992) *Knowledge and Understanding in Art* (London: Oliver and Boyd ISBN 0 050 05086 9)

Kate Stephens (1994) *Learning Through Art and Artefacts* (London: Hodder and Stoughton ISBN 0 340 59683)

Chapter 6 — Strategies and methodologies for teaching art

One of the most persistent myths about teaching art to children is that you have to have a very special collection of personal skills to teach art. This belief is one of the most important reasons for teachers in primary school trying to excuse themselves from attempting to teach art over the years! Like many art coordinators, you may have been confronted with the plaintive cry from colleagues 'I can't teach art because I'm not an artist' or 'because I don't know anything about art'.

One of your most important jobs as the art coordinator is to help and support your colleagues to recognise how they can use the pedagogic skills they have and which they bring to their teaching of other subjects, and how they can apply these teaching skills to the teaching of art.

Looking, talking and seeing

One of the most obvious examples of this application of general teaching skills to the teaching of art is in the way that you can teach children to draw by helping them to 'see' and to observe carefully through using questioning and discussion to focus their looking at familiar things.

Children will see as much through talking about what they can see as through the simple of act of looking. Any teacher can teach children how to draw, simply by using familiar natural and made forms as a starting point and, through using questioning and discussion, to encourage the children to look carefully at what is before them, to observe and talk about what they can see, and to think about how they might draw the forms.

For example, children in Year 1 will be helped in making a drawing of something as familiar as a teddy bear when the teacher intiates the following kind of dialogue about the bear:

> *What shapes can we see?*
> *How big is the body compared with the head?*
> *How big are his ears?*
> *Are they both the same size?*
> *Are the arms bigger, longer, fatter than the legs?*
> *Where do they fit into his body?*
> *How will the teddy bear fit on the page?*
> *Are his eyes darker than his mouth?*
> *Are his eyes bigger than his nose?*
> *Where is the teddy bear smoothest and most hairy?*
> *What patterns do his hairs make? (see Figures 6.1 and 6.2)*

This approach is the foundation for all the teaching of observed drawing in the primary school.

As has already been discussed in the previous section on drawing, the teacher can determine what kind of drawings children will make by using questioning to frame the task of making the drawing. These drawings of teddy bears (Figures 6.1 and 6.2) were made by children whose teacher had **chosen a suitable resource to work from** for five-year-olds (the bear is both simple in its shapes and appearance and appealing to five-year-olds) and who had **focused the children's attention** upon the appearance of the bear and how it might be drawn **through using appropriate questioning**.

FIG 6.1
Teddy bear (Yr 1): fibre tip pen

FIG 6.2
Teddy bear (Yr 2): pencil

Teaching strategies and resources

Teaching strategies

You can help your colleagues to a better undertstanding of the range of teaching strategies they can use to teach art by using the following lists of teaching strategies and of resources, or starting points for making art, as a checklist against their own practice.

Which strategies do they use when teaching art?

What resources do they use as starting points for making art?

How do these strategies and resources interplay with each other?

The most important thing about using such checklists (that follow) for review or discussion with colleagues is to help them to recognise that in teaching art they will use a whole range of teaching methodologies and resources similar to those that they use elsewhere in their teaching of other subjects.

Checklist of strategies and resources for teaching art

Teaching strategies	Teaching resources
exposition (telling them)	images
demonstration	natural forms
questioning	made forms
(teacher based)	the environment
discussion	places
(between teacher and child)	events
interaction/talk	people
(between children)	children
writing	sounds
note taking	music
information collecting	prose and poetry
time	children's work
scale	works of art, craft and design
resource collecting	artists
worksheets	galleries
questionnaires	museums
experimenting	exhibitions
image collecting	

In teaching art, there is a similar interplay between what children will see, respond to and record in their drawings and paintings and what materials they are given to work with as well as the time they are allowed and the scale they are asked to work in.

Useful references

Robert Clement (1993) *The Art Teacher's Handbook: Second Edition* (Cheltenham: Stanley Thornes ISBN 0 7487 1455 3)

Teaching the visual elements of art

As the art coordinator, you can help your colleagues to understand this interplay between making images and using materials and processes by illustrating for them how children are enabled to observe and respond to their experiences more effectively through the teacher choosing the most appropriate materials with which to make the work.

In the National Curriculum, children have to be taught to understand and use the visual elements of art in making their work. They have to be taught how to explore and use the visual elements of **colour**, **line**, **tone**, **pattern**, **texture**, **form**, **shape and space**, but many teachers are uncertain about the procedures for teaching these visual elements of art and it can be helpful to your colleagues if you can find ways to help them identify some simple procedures for doing this.

One obvious starting point is to identify which materials and processes commonly in use in your school are best used to explore and experiment with the visual elements of art, and how such exploration is linked to the choice of suitable starting points or resources.

For example, the drawings of teddy bears were made using pencils or fibre tip pens on white paper. In making these drawings, the children used **line** to record the **shape** of the bears and some shading to explain the different **tones** that they could see.

If the children had been given black, brown and white crayons to draw with on brown paper their drawings of teddy bears would have focused more on the **shapes** and **textures** they could see in the bears.

If they had been asked to paint the teddy bears on grey paper using the primary colours, plus black and white, the focus would have been upon exploring and using the visual elements of **colour** and **shape**.

You can use different materials to help children focus upon different elements within their drawings.

Listed below are those familiar materials for drawing that are available in most primary schools, alongside each one make a list of those visual elements that are best explored using these materials.

It could be useful to include such a list in your art policy documents so that colleagues become familiar with the choices available to them in teaching children about how to use the visual elements of art.

The visual elements of art matched to drawing materials

Biro or fibre tipped pens	e.g.	line	pattern	
Charcoal	e.g.	tone	line	texture
Hard pencils				
Soft pencils				
Coloured pencils				
Wax crayons				
Pastels				
Indian ink				
Chalk				
Coloured felt pens				
Water colour				

Make a list for reference of those visual resource materials you have within your school's collections and indicate alongside these which visual elements will be taught through asking children to make drawings or paintings from these different starting points.

feathers	line	pattern	shape		
skulls	tone	texture	shape	form	
old shoes	line	shape	texture	form	
tea pots	line	shape	pattern	form	colour
views from windows	line	tone	texture	space	colour

You can then encourage colleagues to make cross references between the two lists of materials and resources to encourage them to make appropriate choices when they are planning for their work.

It is important to note that the visual elements of **form** and **space** can only be properly explored when the children are being asked to make studies of familiar made and natural forms from different points of view or where they are asked to record the appearance of things in space.

Chapter 7　Cross-curricular issues

One of the most telling reasons for the introduction and development of the National Curriculum in schools was to rationalise the content of the teaching of the different subjects and through this to eliminate unnecessary repetition and overlap in teaching the knowledge and skills that are characteristic of each subject.

In primary schools, there has been widespread concern that in planning cross-curricular work, teachers did not have a sufficiently clear framework of subject content to ensure that there was a reasonable progression in the teaching of the different subjects from year to year.

Traditionally, art has always had a high profile in cross-curricular work, albeit that this has frequently been because making images has been seen by teachers as a useful way for children to illustrate what has been learnt in other subjects!

An important part of your work as art coordinator is to establish the right balance in your school between the teaching of art as a discipline in its own right and the use of art as an important agent of learning in cross-curricular work.

In good practice, it is self-evident that those schools that demonstrate very high standards in the teaching of art to children are equally those schools where art is used skilfully to enrich and extend learning in cross-curricular work.

Art in its own right

Questions you need to ask of yourself and your colleagues.

What aspects of art does every teacher have to teach to their own class?

Do these provide children with the necessary skills to use art in a variety of ways in other aspects of their work across the curriculum?

Are these basic skills taught sensibly and progressively from year to year?

Do you have enough timetabled time for the specialist teaching of art to deliver the teaching of these basic art skills?

These matters are developed in further in Part 3 Chapter 9 in the section on planning.

Art across the curriculum

In reviewing how you and your colleagues use art in cross-curricular work you need to keep some important principles in mind.

1 The art activities and tasks planned as part of a cross-curricular project must have **value in their own right** and be at an **appropriate level** for the age group concerned.

   For example, children should not be asked to make mechanical copies from pictures of artefacts in association with a history topic, as such an activity does not develop their drawing skills. Rather, they should be asked to work from real artefacts, facsimiles or from reproductions of the work of artists or craftworkers contemporary to the period being studied.

   For example, children in Key Stage 2 should not be asked to make illustrations for stories from 'imagination' but rather through discussing and reviewing the way that other illustrators or artists have explored and dealt with similar themes.

2   Care should be taken to **match the drawing activities** required in cross-curricular work **to the nature of the task** or enquiry to be undertaken. The descriptions of the different purposes for drawing on pp. 66–8 provide a useful framework for identifying natural links between investigation, exploration and the expression of ideas in art and those in other subjects.

3   The match between the Programmes of Study for art and those for other subjects need to be clearly identified to provide guidance for colleagues. These can be included (with examples) in your school's art policy documents.

An outline of the links between art and other subjects

Listed below are some of the working links between art and other subjects, together with some examples in practice. You can construct similar lists based upon practice in your own school.

Language	In the use of vocabulary to describe and compare familiar natural, made and environmental forms *e.g. making a list of words to describe the differences between the appearance of two children in the class before making self portrait drawings.*
	In exploring ideas and feelings about things and events *e.g. through exploring and contrasting the way that artists and poets have described and represented dreams and making their own images of their own dreams.*
History	In examining historical evidence of the way that people lived and worked in other times and cultures *e.g. in Key Stage 1, making studies of the changes that have taken place in the appearance of familiar things in use within the home.*
	In studying the different context within which images are made in different times and cultures *e.g. through comparing the representation of mother and child by artists and craftworkers working in different countries at different times.*

	(where the images are associated with the expression of different kinds of belief and worship, this work will also link effectively with **religious education**)
Science and Geography	Through studying and analysing the changing structure, form and appearance of natural, made and environmental forms *e.g. through analysing the structure of familiar seed heads or in studying the effect of erosion and wear upon made forms within the environment.*
Technology	In using sketch books to investigate source materials and explore ideas for making images and artefacts. In studying and using the visual elements of art in designing and making artefacts *e.g. studying the shapes and colour combinations in plant forms in prepartion for designing and printing fabric materials.* In developing skills in using materials and processes in making images and artefacts which satisfy a particular need *e.g. designing and making plant holders in ceramic materials for use in public parts of the school.*

Planning the teaching of the Programmes of Study for art and other subjects

It is important that you and your colleagues keep a record of what Programmes of Study for other subjects are dealt with through your work in art and vice versa and this is further illustrated in the section on planning in Part 3.

For example, if in your work in history in your school you use historical evidence in support of all the units of history required to be taught in the National Curriculum in Key Stages 1 and 2, you will have gone a long way towards satisfying many of the requirements of the Programmes of Study for Attainment Target 2 in art. Both subjects require that children should be taught to understand the context within which artefacts are made and used and how ideas are expressed through images in different times and cultures.

Useful references

SCDC (1990) *The Arts 5–16, Practice and Innovation* (London: Oliver and Boyd ISBN 0 05 004580 6)

Rob Barnes (1989) *Art, Design and Topic Work* (London: Routledge ISBN 0 415 07826 1)

Robert Clement and Elizabeth Tarr (1992) *A Year in the Art of a Primary School* (NSEAD ISBN 0 904684 11 3)

Chapter 8

Special needs and equal opportunities

Differentiation

Because of the nature of the subject, children of differing abilities find it easier to work on similar tasks than is possible in many other disciplines. Traditionally, in art teaching, differentiation has been established through allowing for individual levels of response to a common task and through the teacher responding to the different levels at which children will work and dealing with their needs individually.

In art where we can accept a variety of appropriate and individual responses from children rather than right or wrong answers, it is a comparatively simple matter to value and support the different levels at which children will draw or paint or model in response to familiar resources and experiences.

Because you can observe the child in the act of making art, it is also easier for you to enter into appropriate and supportive dialogue with the child about the making as it takes place in the classroom. (The use of dialogue to support and monitor children's progress in art is dealt with in more detail on pp. 147–50.)

In Key Stage 1, especially, it is not uncommon for individual children to work with levels of confidence and authority in art that are lacking in their work elsewhere. This is particularly noticeable, for example, in the case of those children who have limited abilities in the use of language but who may communicate their ideas confidently through their work in drawing and painting. For many children with special needs, their work in art will provide valuable support for their early development of communication skills.

Although it would be a rare occasion to differentiate within a group of children by setting them different levels of task in art in Key Stage 1, it may, occasionally be useful to do this in Key Stage 2 and, in particular, to differentiate for the needs of children who are particularly gifted in art and who would benefit from a greater challenge. This can be achieved in a number of ways, as in giving a small group of children within the class more demanding or complex resources to work from, by asking some children to consider more complex issues within work in their critical studies, or by setting individual children demanding tasks appropriate to their needs and level of performance.

Gender

There is no significant difference between the performance of boys and girls in their work in art in their early years in schooling nor is there any particular need to differentiate between the sexes in the setting of tasks and projects within the subject. Although boys and girls will demonstrate different interests and concerns when, for example, they make personal drawings of their own choice in their sketchbooks, both sexes are equally comfortable making work from common starting points and resources.

The main concern regarding gender is in the choice and use of work by artists and craftworkers in relation to the children's work in critical studies in Attainment Target 2. The dominant use in primary schools of the work of the 'Dead white Frenchmen' of the Impressionist and Post-Impressionist schools does require a suitable counterbalance in the selection and use of the work of women artists and designers for study by the children, to ensure that children are properly aware of the contribution that has been made to our cultural development by the work of women artists.

Culture and race

There is a similar need to ensure that children have access to and experience of the work by artists and designers from the many cultural groups represented within our multicultural society.

In some schools, there will be a need to be sensitive to the attitudes of ethnic groups within the school's community towards the representation of certain kinds of images in the work of artists and designers.

Part three Whole school policies
and schemes of work

Chapter 9

Developing an art and design policy

The art policy should provide a framework and a focus for the work in art in your school: it should be both an honest description of your practice in art and demanding enough to encourage colleagues to seek ways to build upon and improve their practice in the teaching of art.

It will need to be accessible to all who will use it and be seen as a supportive working document for colleagues.

The following extract from the *Art Handbook for St Michael's C of E Primary School, Kingsteignton* provides a good summary of the intentions of policy documents for art.

The aims of the *Art Handbook* are:

to deliver the National Curriculum in art;

to provide practical support and advice to teachers in planning and teaching art;

to inform others, such as parents, governors and inspectors about the school's intentions and how it is to deliver its curriculum obligations;

to maintain consistency, continuity and progression throughout the school in teaching art;

to give advice on the efficient management of resources in response to pupils' and curriculum needs;

to keep colleagues informed about each other's work;

to contribute to and support the overall aims and values of the school.

As is also made clear in Part 1, it is essential that producing the policy statements for art for your school should be a shared exercise with colleagues. It is comparatively easy to go to a number of texts or to use your LEA guidelines for art and through these to produce an 'ideal' art policy: it is quite another matter to then persuade colleagues to work to it!

Making an audit of current practice

As part of the process of putting together an art policy, you may need to begin by making an audit of current practice in the teaching of art in your school to identify strengths and weaknesses in current practice and priorities for future planning and INSET.

This can be a very useful way to begin to get colleagues to share their perceptions with you about the subject and the way that they teach it. As an art coordinator with a special interest and well developed skills in the subject, you may well have your own 'ideal' picture of what the art in your school should look like and how it should be taught. If your art policy is to be an honest description of what is taught in your school, you will need to temper your ambitions for the subject with consideration of what your colleagues can reasonably deliver, the extent of their ambitions within their experience of teaching and the limited training that many of them will have had in teaching the subject.

You can undertake an audit by using simple checklists or pro forma to identify what your colleagues have taught or their thinking about different aspects of teaching the subject.

Some examples of these checklists have already been given in Part 2. You could use these checklists with colleagues in order to begin a dialogue about what you would like to achieve in art in your school and what is actually being realised.

As part of the process of making an audit, you can also use checklists to identify what has been taught in art in your school by asking colleagues to make a list of what pupils in their class have experienced over a period of time. It is helpful to make up a simple proforma to complete this kind of review exercise as in the following Figures, 9.1, 9.2 and 9.3.

Suggestion

Consider what kind of audit you need to make of current practice in your school in order to begin dialogue with colleagues about constructing a policy for teaching art. What do you need to know about their practice?

Example of an art audit: 1			
Please complete this chart to show what experiences your class have had in art over the past twelve months			
	Autumn term	Spring term	Summer term
Drawing			
Painting			
Collage/Textiles			
3-D Modelling/ Construction			

FIG 9.1
Proforma for art audit: 1

Example of an art audit: 2			
Please complete this chart to show what experiences your class have had in art over the past twelve months in using the **Visual Elements of Art**			
	Autumn term	Spring term	Summer term
Colour			
Line and tone			
Pattern and texture			
Form, shape and space			

FIG 9.2
Proforma for art audit: 2

Example of an art audit: 3
Which artists', craftworkers' and designers' work have you used with your class over the past year?
Autumn term   Spring term   Summer term

FIG 9.3
Proforma for art audit: 3

© Falmer Press Ltd

A policy for consistency in the practice of teaching art

One of the most effective ways to support progression in teaching art is to seek to establish consistency in the way that the subject is taught throughout your school. Children will only progress in art when they can build making and understanding skills upon their previous experiences in art, therefore your policy must have the establishment of consistency as one of its prior aims.

The diagram below is from the *Art Policy for Thornbury Primary School, Plymouth.* It illustrates the way in which the materials for painting are commonly organised throughout the school. From Reception onwards, children are taught how to use the 'wet brush' method of mixing dry powder colours and because all staff use the same methods and materials for painting from year to year, the children progress rapidly in their abilities to mix, make and apply colour in their work in painting (see Figure 9.4).

Suggestion

Consider other aspects of teaching art where you will need to establish consistency in teaching methods from year to year.

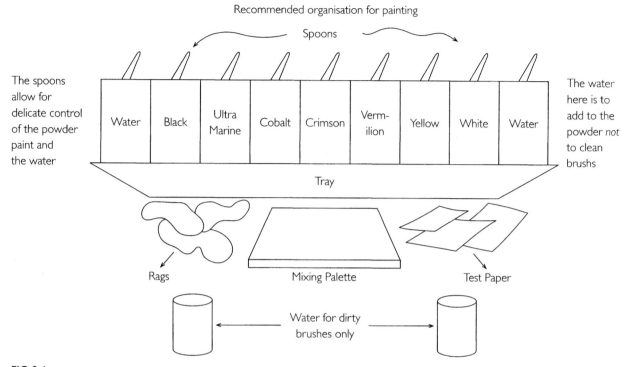

Recommended organisation for painting

Spoons

The spoons allow for delicate control of the powder paint and the water

| Water | Black | Ultra Marine | Cobalt | Crimson | Verm-ilion | Yellow | White | Water |

The water here is to add to the powder *not* to clean brushs

Tray

Rags

Mixing Palette

Test Paper

Water for dirty brushes only

FIG 9.4
Recommended organisation for painting

What form will the policy take?

This is often the first and most daunting question you will have to ask yourself when you begin the task of negotiating and editing a policy for your school. What must it include? What might it include? What form should it take?

You do have access to a considerable body of publications about teaching art in primary schools that have been produced in recent years in response to National Curriculum demands and these will be listed in Part 5. If you work in some LEAs you may already have detailed guidelines for teaching art, usually produced by a working party of teachers led by your LEA art inspector or adviser. You will need to do some preliminary reading to identify what are perceived as being established levels of practice in teaching art and consider how these correspond to expectations in your own school.

In shaping the policy in consultation with colleagues you will need to negotiate a balance between what is ideal and what is practical within the experience and organisation of your own school. Whether you are teaching in a small village school with four staff, or a large urban school with twenty colleagues, you will need to look at existing models and consider how they can be adapted to fit the needs and potential of your own school.

How much the policy will include will also depend upon the skills and experience of colleagues and how much detailed guidance they will need to deliver the pattern of teaching art that the policy determines.

What should the policy include?

The Association for Advisers and Inspectors in Art and Design has recently undertaken a survey of the content of primary school art policies and these are summarised in *Writing an Art Policy and Curriculum Plan for a Primary School* (AAIAD, 1996).

Summary of sections usually included in schools' art policies

1a Rationale for the subject
1b Aims/objectives for art in the school
2   A curriculum outline
3   Methodology for delivery of the subject
4   Teaching style adapted for art
5   Management of the subject
6   How art materials will be organised
7   Equal opportunties
8   The role of differentiation in art activities
9   Assessment — how and when art is assessed
10 Display/presentation — an overall school approach

This is a useful ckecklist to use to begin planning your own policy. You may wish to combine some of these sections, e.g. through combining the sections on methodology and teaching styles, or add others that are particular to the circumstances of your own school, as for example, where you have common policies relating to all the arts or for working with arts workers or institutions within your local community.

Normally, each section of the policy will consist of a number of key points which will describe key aspects of practice within your school and these will be supported by an additional appendix or guideline where necessary, which will provide amplification of detail of the practice.

How much detail you include in the appendices will depend upon the experience and needs of your own colleagues.

If you have a group of colleagues with very varying skills and experience in teaching art you will need to provide more detail in such sections as methods of delivering the art curriculum, because many of them will need specific advice and support in such matters as teaching different forms of drawing or using different methodologies in teaching critical studies.

> Review with colleagues the proposed structure for the art policy in your school
>
> What will be the key sections?
>
> What will be needed by way of supporting appendices or guidelines to enable staff to deliver the art policy for your school?

Statements of intent: aims and objectives

The policy will normally begin with some general statements of intent or what are sometimes fashionably described as 'mission statements'! Frequently this will consist of a number of quotations that will identify why art is important in the education of children and justifying its inclusion within the curriculum.

For example, the policy for St Michael's C of E Primary School, Kingsteignton begins with the following statements:

> Art is a unique and diverse visual language. It is common to all cultures and age groups. Art has a role in its own right but has several functions both to the individual and in playing an inherent communicative and supportive role in every curriculum area, making a significant contribution to the quality of learning.
>
> Art experiences enable children to learn, organise, communicate, express and celebrate, using intuitive as well as logical processes.

Suggestion

The list of aims should be kept as simple and direct as possible, be acceptable as deliverable by your colleagues and be free from art education jargon so that they can be understood and appreciated by parents and governors!

Many schools will use quotations from established authors on art teaching or from such significant reports as Plowden, the Gulbenkian Report *The Arts in Schools* or the National Curriculum Art Working Group report, *Art for Years 5 to 14.*

The aims for the subject

Although the aims for the subject will vary from school to school and will reflect particular strengths or interests present within the school's teaching of art, they will need to incorporate those aims and functions for art teaching that are present within the National Curriculum requirements. It might be useful to refer back to the relevant sections of Part 2 at this point.

Objectives

In some school policies, the general aims and intentions for the teaching of art are further supported by a simple statement about how these aims will be implemented within the general working pattern of the school, for example as at St Michael's C of E Primary School, Kingsteignton where the policy statement includes the following statement of objectives:

Our main objectives are to:

– identify and exploit all suitable opportunities to develop art and design as an entitlement for all pupils;

– provide classroom environments which are conducive to work in art and design;

– provide a full range of tools, materials and resources accessible to all;

– develop and use class/school curriculum planning strategies which incorporate art and design as part of the whole curriculum and relate its work to other subjects;

– plan to allow for continuity and progression in teaching art and design.

The curriculum plan

The art curriculum plan should incorporate the framework for the National Curriculum Orders and be sufficient in detail to show how the Attainment Targets and Programmes of Study for art will be met. This doesn't mean that the art policy has to include the detail of all the Programmes of Study for art but it should have sufficent to show that the framework of Key Strands and Programmes of Study are used to determine the overall plan for your school (see Part 2).

In many school policies the art curriculum plan will consist of an outline of the main themes and areas of work to be explored from year to year as in the two examples below from Thornbury and Stuart Road Primary Schools in Plymouth (Figures 9.5, 9.6, 9.7).

In some schools the outline schemes for work in Art in the curriculum plan are supplemented by more detailed programmes for each year or teaching group as in Figures 9.5 and 9.6.

These examples illustrate how the curriculum plan serves the purpose of providing an outline of work in art for the school so that teachers in each year can see how their work in art contributes to the development of skills, knowledge and understanding in art through the familar pattern of cross-curricular themes.

Cross-curricular issues

As in the examples above, the curriculum plan should give clear guidance as to how the work in art will relate to other curriculum subjects.

Refer back to Part 2, (pp. 88–90) and use this to review with colleagues some of the principles that determine how you teach art, both as a discipline in its own right and where you need to teach it in association with other subjects to their mutual benefit.

The general principles of cross-curricular planning are clearly and simply explained and with good examples in *Planning the Curriculum at Key Stages 1 and 2*, (SCAA, 1995).

Thornbury Primary School Plymouth.
Outline of Themes for Work in Art: Reception to Year 6.

	Autumn	Spring	Summer
R	Myself/Christmas Observational Drawing/Painting Printmaking/3D/Textiles/Ceramics Critical & Contextural Study e.g. Lowry Paintings	Caribbean/Fiction Based Imaginative Drawing/Painting Blocks of colour Printmaking/3D/Textiles/Ceramics Critical & Contextual Study e.g. Klee, Kandinsky	Family Trees Memory drawing/painting Printmaking/3D/Textiles/Ceramics Critical & Contextual Study e.g. Cassatt—families
1	Ourselves/Celebrations/Christmas Observational Drawing/Painting Printmaking/3D/Textiles/Ceramics Critical & Contextural Study e.g. Modigliani/myself	Caribbean/Fiction based Observational Drawing/Painting Fruits Printmaking/3D/Textiles/Ceramics Critical & Contextual Study e.g. Gaugin/Kings & Queens	Houses and Homes Drawing/Painting House from memory Printmaking/3D/Textiles/Ceramics Critical & Contextual Study e.g. Van Gogh's bedroom — painting
2	Victorian (schools) Christmas Observatinal Drawing/Painting Artefacts & Onsite drawing Printmaking/3D/Textiles/Ceramics Critical & Contextual Study e.g. Blocked study on Monet	China/Fiction based Imaginative Drawing/Painting Dragons Printmaking/3D/Textiles/Ceramics Critical & Contextual Study e.g. Chinese Pots/pictures on pots	Movement Drawing/Painting from memory Printmaking/3D/Textiles/Ceramics Critical & Contextual Study e.g. Matisse movement in painting
3	Tavistock/Thornbury Christmas Memory Drawing/Painting — my house Observational work on street furniture. Printmaking/3D/Textiles/Ceramics Critical & Contextural Study Studies of Tavistock	African Country/Fiction based Imaginative painting — colours of Africa Observational Drawing of artefacts Printmaking/3D/Textiles/Ceramics Critical & Contextual Study e.g. Muafangengo/Tony Hudson	Ancient Eygpt Observational Drawing/Painting — Artefacts Printmaking — pattern in Eygpt 3D/Ceramics/Textiles Critical & Contextual Study e.g. Egyptian Art
4	Invaders/Settlers/Christmas Celtic Patterns. Observational drawing Image drawing from description and painting Printmaking/3D/Textiles/Ceramics Critical & Contextural Study e.g. study — Personal Portraits	Brazil/Fiction based Observational drawing/painting of plants/foliage. Imaginative painting Printmaking/3D/Textiles/Ceramics Critical & Contextual Study e.g. Rousseau	Ships and Seafarers Observational Drawing/Painting — Sea artefacts Imaginative Painting — The Sea pirates etc Printmaking/3D/Textiles/Ceramics Critical & Contextual Study e.g. Contemporary artists
5	Tudors/Stuarts/Christmas Observational drawing/painting Printmaking/3D/Textiles/Ceramics Critical & Contextural Study e.g. Tudor Portraits/Brueghel	Japan/Fiction based Imaginative Drawing/Painting Printmaking/3D/Textiles/Ceramics Critical & Contextual Study e.g. Housoukai, Japanese Art	Plymouth (The Blitz) Observational Drawing/Painting — Landmarks Printmaking/3D/Textiles/Ceramics Critical & Contextual Study e.g. Beryl Cook, Chris Robinson, Henry Moore — War Artists
6	Victorians/Industry/Christmas Observational & Imaginative Drawing/Painting Printmaking/3D/Textiles/Ceramics Critical & Contextual Study e.g. William Morris, Pre-Raphaelites	India/Ancient Greece Observational Drawing/Painting — Patterns of India. Printmaking — India Pattern 3D/Textiles/ceramics Critical & Contextual Study Pattern on vessels e.g. Clarisse Cliff, Greek Pots etc	Dartmoor/European Community Imaginative Studies on rivers — myths Printmaking/3D/Textiles/Ceramics Critical & Contextual Study e.g. Widgery/contemporary collection

FIG 9.5
Art curriculum plan

Stuart Road Primary School, Plymouth.
Outline Schemes for Work in Art, Key Stage 2

Stuart Road Primary School — Outline Scheme of Work for Art

Key Stage 2 Year 3/4 — Rolling Programme Year One

Term: Autumn	Term: Spring	Term: Summer
Time Allocation: 12 hours	Time Allocation: 11 hours	Time Allocation: 13 hours
Central Themes Science: Grouping and classifying materials Geography: Rivers, weather, settlement, environmental change. Place: Local area History: Local history, change of landscape after WW2. Civil war — Plymouth. Tudor Trade Linked Art Theme: Plymouth/The Sea/Fishing Key Skills Development: DRAWING/ PAINTING/ CERAMICS Key Critical Studies: ARTISTS FROM THE WEST COUNTRY INCLUDING CONTEMPORARY WORK: THE NEWLYN SCHOOL; BEACHES IN ART; TURNER'S SEASCAPES; FISH IN DESIGN	Central Themes: Science: Light and sound History: Britain since 1930 or Victorian Britain Linked Art Theme: Britain since 1930/Victorians Key Skills Development: DRAWING/PRINTING Key Critical Studies: SCOPE FOR FOCUS ON WAR ARTISTS — HENRY MOORE/PAUL NASH or VICTORIAN ARTISTS AND DESIGNERS; VICTORIAN FANTASY — RICHARD DADD; FOCUS ON INTERIORS AND INTERIOR DESIGN	Central Themes: Science: Green plant as organisms. Growth and nutrition. Living things — adaptation Geography: Environmental change. Rivers, weather. Place: Selected Environments Linked Art Theme: Plants Key Skills Development: DRAWING/ COLLAGE/ FABRIC WORK Key Critical Studies: PLANTS IN ANY MEDIUM AND FROM A VARIETY OF CULTURES; USE OF PLANTS FOR DESIGN PAST AND PRESENT

Key Stage 2 Year 3/4 — Rolling Programme Year 2

Term: Autumn	Term: Spring	Term: Summer
Time Allocation: 12 hours	Time Allocation: 11 hours	Time Allocation: 13 hours
Central Themes: Science: Changing Materials, separating mixtures of materials Geography: Rivers, weather, settlement, environmental change. Place: Dartmoor Linked Art Theme: Landscapes Key Skills Development: DRAWING/ PAINTING/ CERAMICS Key Critical Studies: LANDSCAPE IN ANY KIND OF ART FROM ANY TIME OR CULTURE. LOCAL WATER-COLOUR ARTISTS. CONTEMPORARY CERAMICS	Central Themes: Science: Simple circuits, Forces and Motion History: Life in Tudor Times Linked Art Theme: Tudors Key Skills Development: DRAWING/ PAINTING/ PRINTING Key Critical Studies: PORTRAITS OF PEOPLE OVER TIME IN ANY MEDIUM. FOCUS ON TUDOR PORTRAITS AND ARTISTS PARTICULARLY HOLBEIN.	Central Themes: Science: Humans as organisms. Life processes, nutrition, circulation. Geography: Settlement, weather. Place Global/local contexts Linked Art Theme: Weather Key Skills Development: DRAWING/ FABRIC COLLAGE Key Critical Studies: WEATHER IN PAINTING PARTICULARLY SCENES FROM OTHER CULTURES: WORK OF GAUGUIN

Key Stage 2 Year 5/6 — Rolling Programme Year 1

Term: Autumn	Term: Spring	Term: Summer
Time Allocation: 12 hours	Time Allocation: 11 hours	Time Allocation: 13 hours
Central Themes Science: Simple circuits, Forces and Motion Geography: Rivers, weather, settlement, environmental change. Place: Developing Country Linked Art Theme: Colour and Light Key Skills Development: DRAWING/ FABRIC COLLAGE Key Critical Studies: CONTRAST THE STYLES OF ARTISTS WHO USED COLOUR AS A FEATURE OF THEIR WORK: IMPRESSIONISTS, MATISSE, MONDRIAN, WARHOL, LEGER, PICASSO, PARTICULARLY 20TH CENTURY ARTISTS.	Central Themes: Science: Changing materials. Separating mixtures of materials History: Ancient Egypt Maya or Aztecs Linked Art Theme: Egypt, Maya or Aztecs Key Skills Development: DRAWING/ PAINTING Key Critical Studies: FOCUS ON ARTEFACTS FROM CHOSEN ANCIENT CULTURE, PARTICULARLY DRESS, DECORATION, JEWELLERY, PAINTINGS.	Central Themes: Science: Green plants — reproduction. Health, Living things — feeding, micro-organisms Geography: Rivers, weather. Place: Selected Environments/localities Linked Art Theme: Rivers or Water Key Skills Development: DRAWING/ CERAMICS Key Critical Studies: WEATHER IN WESTERN ART CONTRASTED WITH THAT OF NON-WESTERN CULTURES. WORK OF GAUGUIN.

Key Stage 2 Year 5/6 — Rolling Programme Year 2

Term: Autumn	Term: Spring	Term: Summer
Time Allocation: 12 hours	Time Allocation: 11 hours	Time Allocation: 13 hours
Central Themes Science: Vibration & Sound The Earth & Beyond Periodic Changes Geography: Rivers, weather, settlement, environmental change. Place: Europe. History: Ancient Greece Linked Art Theme: Ancient Greece Key Skills Development: DRAWING/ PRINTING/ SCULPTURE Key Critical Studies: ARTEFACTS OF ANCIENT GREECE — CERAMICS, SCULPTURE, BUILDINGS; MOVEMENT IN ART — ATHLETES, DANCERS.	Central Themes: Science: Grouping and Classifying Materials Geography: Characteristic effect of human activity Place: UK History: Romans, Anglo Saxons or Vikings Linked Art Theme: Art in the Built Environment Key Skills Development: DRAWING/ CERAMICS/ 3D/ FABRIC WORK Key Critical Studies: INDUSTRIAL LANDSCAPES, ARCHITECTS; WORK OF LOWRY AND PAUL KLEE	Central Themes: Science: Humans as organisms, circulation, movement, growth, reproduction, health. Linked Art Theme: People and/or Animals Key Skills Development: DRAWING/ PAINTING/ FABRIC COLLAGE/ SCULPTURE Key Critical Studies: PEOPLE/ANIMALS IN ART FROM A VARIETY OF CULTURES — GROUPS OF PEOPLE, FAMILIES, WORK OF STUBBS, JAPANESE PAINTING (FISH PARTICULARLY) HOGARTH, GAINSBOROUGH

FIG 9.6
Outline scheme of work for art

Stuart Road Primary School — Draft Curriculum Mapping for Art

Key Stage 2   Year 3/4   Rolling Programme Year One

Term: Autumn Time Allocation: 12 hours	Term: Spring Time Allocation: 11 hours	Term: Summer Time Allocation: 13 hours
Central Themes Science: Grouping and classifying materials Geography: Rivers, weather, settlement, environmental change. Place: Local area History: Local history, change of landscape after WW2. Civil war — Plymouth. Tudor Trade	Central Themes: Science: Light and sound History: Britain since 1930 or Victorian Britain	Central Themes: Science: Green plants as organisms. Growth and nutrition. Living things — adaptation Geography: Environmental change. Rivers, weather. Place: Selected Environments
Linked Art Theme: Plymouth/The Sea/Fishing Key Skills Development: DRAWING/ PAINTING/ CERAMICS Key Critical Studies: ARTISTS FROM THE WEST COUNTRY INCLUDING CONTEMPORARY WORK; THE NEWLYN SCHOOL; BEACHES IN ART; TURNER'S SEASCAPES; FISH IN DESIGN	Linked Art Theme: Britain since 1930/Victorians Key Skills Development: DRAWING/ PRINTING Key Critical Studies: SCOPE FOR FOCUS ON WAR ARTISTS — HENRY MOORE/PAUL NASH or VICTORIAN ARTISTS AND DESIGNERS; VICTORIAN FANTASY — RICHARD DADD; FOCUS ON INTERIORS AND INTERIOR DESIGN	Linked Art Theme: Plants Key Skills Development: DRAWING/ COLLAGE/ FABRIC WORK Key Critical Studies: PLANTS IN ANY MEDIUM AND FROM A VARIETY OF CULTURES; USE OF PLANTS FOR DESIGN PAST AND PRESENT
Key Learning Objectives Investigating & Making: ■ select and record from direct experiences and first hand observation; ■ collect and use visual evidence using a sketchbook; ■ experiment with and develop control of tools and techniques in ceramics, drawing and painting; ■ make a functional piece of ceramic work; ■ experiment with colour, line and texture; ■ reflect on their work and suggest modifications for the future.	Key Learning Objectives Investigating & Making: ■ select and record from direct experiences and first hand observation; ■ collect and use visual evidence using a sketchbook; ■ experiment with and develop control of tools and techniques in drawing and printing; ■ design and make a printed artefact; ■ experiment with colour in printing; shape and form in drawing; ■ reflect on their work and suggest modifications for the future.	Key Learning Objectives Investigating & Making: ■ select and record from direct experiences and first hand observation; ■ collect and use visual evidence using a sketchbook; ■ experiment with and develop control of tools and techniques in drawing and fabric collage; ■ design and make a textile artefact; ■ experiment with colour, line and tone in drawing and colour and texture in fabric work; ■ reflect on their work and suggest modifications for the future.

FIG 9.7
Draft curriculum mapping for art

Chapter 10

Implementing the policy

Your school's art policy should provide some guidance as to how the art curriculum is to be delivered in your school. This may include reference to a number of issues including:

■ the use of time and staff expertise;

■ the required balance and content of the art curriculum;

■ what general learning experiences the children will achieve through their work in art;

■ what range of teaching methodologies staff will use in their teaching of the subject;

■ common policies for planning work in art;

■ how progression is to be achieved from year to year.

The main purpose of this section is to establish how you intend to put into practice the principles established through your statement of intentions and your curriculum plan.

Learning experiences

For example, the art policy for St Michael's C of E Primary School, Kingsteignton, includes the following statement about what general learning experiences the children will experience through their work in art:

Learning experiences offered in art should provide pupils with the opportunity to:

– be encouraged through experimentation and investigation to select materials, technology, skills and tools appropriate to the task in hand;

– be encouraged to create and express, recount and communicate in different media to a variety of audiences;

– manage their own time and meet the challenge of completing assignments;

– be encouraged to reflect on current work and to predict and plan a subsequent stage, building on mistakes and successes.

Content and balance

In some schools, the content and balance of the proposed art curriculum is described in very general terms:

The art course will provide pupils with opportunties to:

develop observational skills;

extend their powers of personal expression;

acquire confidence and skills in using a wide range of tools, media and processes;

develop an understanding of the use of the visual elements of art;

acquire the capacity to evaluate their own and other artists' work.

In some schools the content and balance of the programme of work in art is specifically defined as in the policy statement in the art policy for Thornbury Primary School, Plymouth.

Balance should be maintained within the range of media and experiences defined by the School Art Policy

The following is defined as the minimum:

all modes if drawing should be covered in a year — NB good observational work is **essential** in each term;

a good quality painting should be achieved twice a year;

printmaking should be achieved once a year;

a ceramic module once a year;
a textile experience once a year;*
a 3D construction once a year.*

* These activities may overlap with design technology.
They need only happen once across the two subjects.

At least once a year children should experience a complete critical
and contextual study of an artist or a school of artists.

Use of time and teacher expertise

This section may include reference to the time allocated to
the teaching of art in Key Stages 1 and 2 and the distinction
between the discrete time given to teaching children the basic
skills and understanding necessary to the subject, and that
additional cross-curricular time where they are using their art
skills in association with learning in other subjects.

Some schools have more specific policies for the use of
concentrated time for the teaching of art, especially in Key
Stage 2 and where it may be recognised that it will be to the
pupil's advantage to have longer and more concentrated
periods of time allocated to the teaching of art to allow them
opportunties to work in more depth and to complete a more
complex task in an extended session.

In most schools, the children's programme of work in art is
taught entirely by the class teacher. Where you are making use
of particular teacher expertise in art, as in the leadership of a
year group in larger schools, or the use of teachers with special
skills to teach classes other than their own, you will need to
indicate this in your policy. The use of particular expertise,
where one teacher will deliver the teaching of work in textiles
in one Key Stage through working alongside colleagues or
with groups of children extracted from a class, should be
indicated, too.

If you are fortunate enough to have parents or friends of the
school who are practising artists or craftworkers who regularly
contribute their expertise to supporting the teaching of groups
of children in your school, it is useful to indicate this in your
policy statements.

Methodologies

In your general statement about the teaching styles and methodologies to be used in teaching art, it will be sufficient to state that a variety of methodologies appropriate to the subject will be employed and that these might range from using didactic and structured teaching of drawing to using investigative methods and systems to pursue ideas and solve problems.

Depending upon the level of expertise and experience amongst your colleagues, you may wish to include more specfic advice through the use of appendices to remind colleagues of the variety of methodologies that can be used in teaching art (see pp. 79–86).

Planning

In most schools, there are now in place agreed strategies or frameworks for planning the delivery of the National Curriculcum both in the long-, medium- and short-term.

In putting together your art policy, you will need to consider adopting an agreed framework for colleagues to use in planning, recording and monitoring the work they undertake in art with their own classes. The framework should aim for balance: it should be simple to use yet contain sufficient detail for them to be able to plan projects based on the National Curriculum guidelines on art.

You could usefully begin by returning to the framework for the Attainment Targets and Programmes of Study for the National Curriculum in art and review with colleagues how these might determine the form your planning should take (DfEE 1992) (pp. 39–40).

Suggestion

Planning frameworks can take a variety of forms and it will be useful to look at and compare a number used in different schools and LEAs, and to discuss wih colleagues which model might best serve the needs of your own school or be adapted to your own use.

You will see that when planning art projects you will need to take account of how the following key aspects are incororated into your planning framework:

1. What investigations and activities will take place to explore experiences and ideas relevant to the topic?
2. What resources are needed to focus the investigation?
3. What materials and processes will be used?

4   Which visual elements of art will be studied?
5   Which artists, designers and craftworkers should be studied to reinforce the children's understanding of the theme?

Compare the following three examples of planning frameworks and consider how well these work in relation to the questions above and how they might correspond to your own ideas for designing a planning framework for use in your school (Figures 10.1, 10.2, 10.3).

Progression

Some schools include a brief summary in their art policy of the stages that children go through in making their work as in Chapter 5.

In many schools's policies and in all LEA guidelines for the subject, will include detailed descriptions of the progression that children should make in working with the different materials and processes used in art and of the development in their understanding and use of the visual elements of art.

These are discussed and illustrated in the following section and you will need to review with colleagues how similar descriptions of progression might be used as appendices to your own art policy and in how much detail they need to be presented in order to meet the needs of your own school.

Continuity and progression

This section of your art policy will consist of a number of appendices in which you will detail how you will order the teaching and learning in a number of key processes in the work in art and design in your school.

These will include such key activities as drawing and painting and the detail of such additional processes that are taught throughout Key Stages 1 and 2 in your school.

INDIVIDUAL PROJECT PLANNING SHEET

Context	Area of Study	Tasks, Activities and Experiences	Resources	Classroom Organisation and Teaching Style	Review and Assessment Opportunities	Links with Other Subjects
■ cross-curricular or topic related ■ discrete art	■ exploring the visual and tactile elements — line, shape, colour, tone, pattern, form, texture, space	■ investigating, e.g. use of sketchbook, collecting source material ■ recording from observation ■ using memory and imagination ■ expressing ideas and feelings ■ processes, e.g. drawing, painting, printing, modelling, constructing, textiles, photography etc.	■ stimulus — displays, books, videos, visits ■ source material — first hand, second hand ■ examples of artists, craftworkers and designers' work — original or reproduction ■ materials & tools ■ teaching support	■ pupil groupings ■ teaching and learning strategies ■ differentiation ■ equal opportunities etc.	■ display, sketchbooks, teacher observations, discussions, written explanations, presentation at assembly etc.	

National Curriculum PoS

FIG 10.1
Essex LEA Art and Design Curriculum Handbook; Individual project planning sheet

Art and Design — A Primary Framework
Planning Schedule for an art focus within a topic

Project/Theme		Class	Age Group	Date
Ourselves			6 to 7 years	

Possible Art Activities
- Observational drawing and painting. Portraiture, self-portraits.
- Observing how the body moves, its form and proportion.
- Expressive work in dance and costumes linked in with experience of new materials.

Activities	Elements			
	Perceptual	Personal	Social/Cultural	Exploring Materials and Visual Language
■ Exploring Materials	Observing ourselves in mirrors.	Drawing facial expressions.	Looking at images of the children's families & themselves.	Mark making using pencil, pastel, chalk.
■ Portraits	Discussing what we see, how our faces can change. Movement lesson.	Drawing our portraits. Experiencing movements.	Looking at artist's self-portraits and painting in the same way.	Combining materials for different effects.
■ Modelling with Clay	Focus exploration on body shapes. Draw round bodies and photograph to record.	Open and closed shapes. Choosing postures to model in clay.	Look at pictures of dancers from different cultures.	Exploring paint with reference to different artist's styles.
■ Narrative Painting	Looking at playtime activities and sketching them.	Painting ourselves at play.	Look at Brueghel's painting: 'Children at Play.'	Modelling with clay to emphasise form/ shape. Colour matching using playground colours.

Resources	Materials
■ Artists' self-portraits. ■ Brueghel's painting 'Children at Play'. Mirrors, Cameras. ■ Pictures of dancers from other cultures.	Pencils, pastels, chalk, paper, clay, powder paints of redimix. (3 primary colours + black & white)

Organisation
- Order resources from library and museum service.
- Encourage children to bring in photographs. Collect supporting illustrations. Make an introductory display for discussion.
- Structure activities to include mark-making with materials, looking, focusing, reflecting, recording, developing with materials.

Development
Clay portraits. Designing our own games and dances.
Making costumes and disguising ourselves.

FIG 10.2
Planning schedule for art within the topic 'Ourselves'

Bearing in mind that the National Curriculum requires that children should work in both two- and three-dimensional design in each Key Stage you will need to consider which craft and design processes will be the focus for your design-based work and how these relate to your work in technology.

Stuart Road Primary School — Curriculum Planning

Subject: ART	Year Group/s: 2	Class: 3	Term: Autumn 1996
Theme: *Kings and Queens* Key Learning Objectives Investigating & Making: ■ select and record from direct experiences and first hand observation; ■ select and sort visual evidence using a sketchbook where appropriate; ■ experiment with and develop control of tools and techniques in painting, drawing and fabric collage; ■ make a non functional piece of fabric work; ■ experiment with colour, line and texture; ■ reflect on their work and suggest modifications for the future. Key Learning Objectives Knowledge & Understanding: ■ identify portraits in the school and the locality; ■ recognise similarities and differences in portraits from different times; ■ recognise how artists have used colour, line and texture in their work; ■ identify and describe works of art studied in simple terms.		Central Themes *Science:* Human body *Geography:* Local environment *History:* Changes in People — family; people in the past	

Pupil Activities	Scheme of Work Checklist	Unit time: 12 hours
	Key Skills Development: DRAWING/PAINTING/FABRIC WORK Drawing: Add the materials requiring greater control: chalk, charcoal and biro, to the range introduced at Reception. Painting: Powder colour and agreed method of working. Water-colour boxes for fine work towards end of Yr2. The emphasis in the National Curriculum is on exploring colour mixing. Collect, sort and classify colours both primary and secondary. Match colours carefully with observed stimulus. Work from a limited palette & use black and white. Mixing primary and secondary colours including brown. Making as many different tones of one colour as possible. Lightening colour without using white. Darkening colours without using black. Building colour environments. Fabric Work: Children should have access to different textured fabrics and threads. Explore textures through fabric and create fabric collages using cut shapes and glue initially. Begin some simple appliqué — attaching fabrics with the running stitch. Build up a piece of work using stitching and gluing. All work in this sequence can either be on a group or individual basis. Begin with simple weaving work using a card loom, rags and paper. Through this activity the children should be encouraged to match and choose the colours appropriate to the task. **Express** ideas and feelings **Record** observations **Design and make** artefacts **Explore 2D and 3D media** **Gather and use** resources to develop ideas **Select and sort visual evidence and information — use sketchbooks where appropriate** **Key Critical Studies:** PORTRAITS OF ROYALTY OVER TIME FROM PAINTING MINIATURES TO PHOTOGRAPHY OF THE PRESENT DAY	

FIG 10.3
Curriculum planning framework: 'Kings and Queens'

Review with colleagues how you intend to deliver the teaching of such design-based areas as textiles, print-making and ceramics and which of these will need to be included in your art policy to provide guidance to all teachers for the teaching of these disciplines.

Mapping the key processes in art and design

The appendices dealing with the teaching of the key processes in art and design need to be kept as simple as possible, with sufficient detail to provide colleagues with a general picture of how the teaching of each of these processes will develop from year to year and so that they can use them as a framework for their own teaching.

Consider the examples below and review with colleagues how they correspond to your own teaching of these processes and how similar outlines of the development of children's learning in key processes might be structured for use in your own school (Figures 10.4, 10.5, 10.6, 10.7).

PLANNING FOR PROGRESSION IN ART AND DESIGN

Practices and Materials *Drawing*

Year	Practice	Materials	Activity
R/I	Exploring materials and mark-making, smudging, blending and overlaying. Beginning to use observation	A range of pencils, chalks, pastels, wax crayons, white or coloured paints	Exploratory drawing, scribbling, first pictures of a person of object
2	Experimenting with tools and materials and drawing from observation	Hard and soft pastels, pencils, coloured pencils and chalks. Black paper	Draw familiar places or things, such as people houses or objects such as the skeleton
3	Represent ideas and images matched to the pupils' own world and experiences	Pencils and a variety of drawing tools. White paper	Draw familiar objects or things related to a set theme such as musical instruments
4	Further matching of their work to the natural and made world concentrating on line, tone, size, proportion and detail	A range of pencils, coloured pencils or other drawing tools. White paper	Draw a friend dressed in a Tudor costume
5	Observational study of the natural and made world concentrating on colour, tone, scale, space and recession	Coloured pastels on black or grey paper	Draw plants and flowers in the school garden focusing on colour mixing and analysis
6	Further observational study concentrating on the full range of visual elements and personal expression	Coloured pastels on black or grey paper	Draw a range of natural or made forms from observation in the classroom

FIG 10.4
Planning for progression in art and design: drawing

Somerset Art and Design
ACTIVITY: DRAWING KS1 SUMMARY DIAGRAM — YEARS 1 & 2

At the beginning of this stage children will be at a wide range of levels of attainment in drawing skills.

Some will hardly have moved beyond naming their scribbles. Others will already have well-developed schema with which to depict and analyse their world.

The schema and their development dominate these years but children can make observational drawings if they are encouraged to look closely before they draw.

Fundamental to this stage is the direct use of a variety of tools and materials for mark-making. Always based on an experimental point of view, this work moves from pure play to more structured exercises.

	PERCEPTUAL	PERSONAL	SOCIAL/CULTURAL	VISUAL LANGUAGE AND USE OF MATERIALS
	Drawing natural and made objects	Drawing myself, my family, my pets	Make a beginning on drawings that convey information and explanation. This can include diagrams and simple plans	Playing with drawing materials
	Use questions to encourage careful observation	Drawings to tell a story about me	Sequences of drawings to tell a story or explain how something works	Clay, fabric, pens, pencils, markers, brushes, paper, card
	Draw in 3 dimensions using clay, textiles, paper and card to respond to natural and made objects	Drawing things I particularly like	Drawings that are stimulated by drama and role play	Finding out how many different marks are possible with tools and materials
	Look closely at a part of a person, animal or object, try to draw exactly what is seen there	Drawings that express and explain how I feel about things		Building up drawings from specific shapes
		Illustrating a story that I particularly like		Drawing heavily, lightly, delicately, roughly
				Using found materials — e.g. sticks, sand — to draw with
UNDERSTANDING ART AND DESIGN	Look at and talk about observational drawings by other people.	Look at drawings of people from other times, talk about them. Do drawings of ourselves for people to look at in the future. What were people telling us in their drawings about their likes and dislikes and about their feelings?	How did people draw at other times? How do they draw in other cultures? Look and talk about drawings with different contents.	Looking at the range of marks in other people's drawings made with different tools e.g. cave paintings, stick drawings, pencil, pen, etc.

FIG 10.5
Framework and Programmes of Study Years 1 and 2: Drawing Somerset LEA.

In many ways paint presents considerably more problems than other media and is frequently mis-used or un-used in many circumstances. Powder paint is a versatile medium giving the opportunity for sensitive colour mixing to every child. Tuition and tasks should be given in colour mixing so that every painting is an exercise in colour mixing. To explore and develop colour awareness takes time and it must therefore be expected than children will need time to complete work. Powder paints are avoided by some teachers because they are thought to be messy and a nuisance but thoughtful organisation can prevent most hazards and make it possible for children to work in good order.

Age Group	Materials to introduce	Experiences with Colour
KS1	Powder colour and agreed method of working. Water-colour boxes for fine work towards end of Yr2.	The emphasis in the National Curriculum is on **exploring colour mixing.** Collect, sort and classify colours both primary and secondary. Match colours carefully with observed stimulus. Work from a limited palette & use black and white. Mixing primary and secondary colours including brown. Making as many different tones of one colour as possible. Lightening colour without using white. Darkening colours without using black. Building colour environments. Colour in works of art: Use the Impressionists; Expressionists and other works where colour is a main feature, e.g. Picasso's blue period, Degas' Group of Dancers (greens).
KS2 Yr3 & 4	Wet paper water-colour. Using inks.	The emphasis in the National Curriculum is on applying colour mixing. Recognising and mixing intermediate colours. Working with one colour against a variety of backgrounds. Look at variety of intermediate colours in works of art. Observational painting of groups of objects with similar colour ranges. Mixing from memory. Working with one colour, black and white.
KS2 Yr5 & 6		Provide further opportunities for children to apply their knowledge of colour mixing. Investigate the properties of complementary colours. Continue to use works of art as a reference. At this stage children should be able to select the materials they need and execute a painting which may take some time to complete.

FIG 10.6
Developing Painting Skills: Art Policy, Stuart Road Primary School

KS2

Painting Media	Children should	Possible activities/starting points	Possible topic links	Notes
Range of brushes, inks, powder and blocks, redimix, dyes, natural pigments such as onions and berries.	Extend colour mixing to sundry and tertiary colours.	Possible starting points/activities.	Colour and light.	Emphasis should be on drawing with a brush as much as using paint to 'colour in'.
	Observe and reproduce colours in natural/manmade objects.	Make as many different reds/blues etc as possible. Try to make black.	Pattern and shape.	
	Extend experience of colour and tone, blending and stippling.	Examine the effect of white on different colours.	Surfaces/materials.	Language; e.g. implement, technique, expressive, balance, combination, texture, tone, shade, abstract, landscape, portrait.
	Explore expression in painting — emotions, moods, atmosphere.	Discuss shades of colour (e.g.: paint charts).	Local Environment.	
	Apply paint with many different tools and to different surfaces and begin to have confidence in selecting appropriate tool for a task.	Look at different tones of colour: e.g. sky blue, sea blue, cornflower blue. See how many scraps of cloth of the same colour you can find.	'Changes'. 'Water' Air/Flight	
	Apply knowledge to solve problems.	Sort material — strongest to palest. Record contrasting colours.	History theme — look at relevant artists' work.	
	Return to and refine a painting.	Look at seasonal colours in the environment.		
	Develop associated language.	Look at colour from other parts of the world; e.g. Australian landscape.		
	Use paint for different purposes.	Look at paintings and see how artists have used colour to express mood.		
	LATER KS2	Discuss use of colour in posters.		
	Refine concepts relative to colour.	Match colours to a magazine picture, a natural object, scraps of fabric/paper.		
	Make wide use of techniques of applying paint to different surfaces.	Move from red to blue in gradual steps.		
	Become independent in selecting techniques and materials to use in a painting.	Paint small areas of a still life composition.		
	Throughout KS2, children should be looking at and discussing the work of artists and discussing art generally.	Look at artists work — use technique. Paint in the style, use colours. Observe the environment. Explore different ways we use paint; e.g. house paint.		

FIG 10.7
Painting: Key Stage 2 — Hand book for Art and Design in the Primary School (East Sussex LEA)

The visual elements of art

You will also need to consider whether you should include within your art policy some guidance as to the way in which the teaching of the use and understanding of the visual elements of art is structured and developed.

Although there is considerable overlap between teaching children the use of materials and processes and understanding of the visual elements of art, as in the teaching of painting and the acquisition of the language of colour, it may be helpful to colleagues to draw their attention to the way in which use of the visual elements progresses.

Consider and compare the three examples from guidelines below which illustrate different ways in which progression in the teaching of the visual elements of art can be described and consider how they relate to the needs of your own colleagues (Figures 10.8, 10.9, 10.10).

The first two, from Stuart Road Primary School and Barking and Dagenham LEA, illustrate useful ways to describe continuity in teaching the visual elements of art in Key Stages 1 and 2 and the third, from Durham LEA, shows the overall relationship between teaching the visual elements of art in drawing and other areas of the art and design curriculum.

Some guidance on developing line, shape and form, texture and pattern: Art Policy, Stuart Road Primary School

At Key Stage 1

Line	Shape and Form	Texture	Pattern
Look at different qualities of line — thick, thin, wavy, straight and use a variety of media to make different lines Look at the outlines of objects and draw them Look at the way lines change direction in different objects and draw them carefully	Identify simple shapes and forms using the appropriate language. Observe and draw simple shapes. Look at shapes in the natural and man made world	Identify different textures — smooth, rough, etc. Analyse the surfaces of object and interpret in different media, e.g. the surface of a teddy bear in charcoal or with felt pens. Experiment with mark-making using different media	Observe pattern in the natural and manmade environments. Identify and create repeat patterns and random patterns

At Key Stage 2 (Yrs 3 & 4)

Line	Shape and Form	Texture	Pattern
Experiment with varying thicknesses of line to suggest form and shadow	Observe and draw more complex shapes and forms from natural and manmade objects	Identify and draw the effect of light on a surface. Choose appropriate media to represent more complex textures in natural and manmade objects	Create more complex patterns e.g. alternating and half drop

At Key Stage 2 (Yrs 5 & 6)

Line	Shape and Form	Texture	Pattern
Identify and use horizontal, vertical, diagonal and curved lines for direction Look for implied lines in design	Observe and draw the effect of light on a form using a variety of techniques	Use a variety of techniques to interpret the texture of a surface	Observe and create rhythmical patterns, border and band patterns using a variety of media

FIG 10.8
Developing line, shape and form: Texture and pattern in Key Stage 1

ART VISUAL ELEMENTS

The guidance is described by reference to the elements of art. This does not assume that schools structure their KS2 art schemes on these elements as discrete units. This is a check list to ensure that the elements of art as described in the National Curriculum Art document are addressed. Schools will need to ensure that pupils experience a good range of two and three dimensional work and that work ranges from observational recording to broadly imaginative and expressive pieces.

	'VISUAL ELEMENTS'								Talking & writing about art (Inc. gallery visit)
	Line	Tone	Colour	Texture	Pattern	Shape	Form	Space	
Year 3	(Edge) Use outline in drawing. Develop rhythms in line/pattern (string printing)	Use black and white and mixed greys to create monochrome picture	Use 3 primary colours plus white to create a range of hues and shades. Paint from observed objects with colour accuracy	Use stippling techniques, sponges, etc. to create textural effects. Use rubbings to record textures and collage them into pictorial composition	Develop simple repeat serial patterns (stamps/print) Stitch line patterns	Record simple observed shapes (regular and irregular)	Assemble found objects into sculpture to explore solid forms (boxes, tubes)	Organise the shapes of objects within a visualised space using large and small to indicate distance	Look at and describe a single image or object
Year 4	(Surface) Use line to show surface features and details of objects	Use gradations of tone in primary colours	Develop an understanding of the moods related to colours	Use pencil and other mark-making instruments to create textural effects in drawing	Develop symmetrical repeat patterns (drawn/collaged)	Draw natural shapes in relation to their underlying forms	Model simple solid and hollow forms (clay; papier mache)	Use background and foreground to structure elements within a picture	Compare and contrast two images or objects
Year 5	(Volume) Use line to describe the 3D character of objects	Use tone to illustrate light and shade of objects	Use a 'double primary' palette. Make gradations of warm and cool hues. Develop use of transparent colour washes	Compose arrangements of textures from textiles (sewn, appliqué/collage)	Develop interlinked repeat patterns (design stamps/blocks)	Compose shapes into pictorial space (picture plane)	Combine found and created forms to express sculptural idea	Use background, middle and foreground to structure a picture. Identify, through observation, lines of natural perspective	Discuss reasons why the artist made the work of art
Year 6	Use hard and soft lines to describe quality of edges or appearance	Use gradated tone to describe 3D character of objects	Create sense of visual depth by employing cool and warm colours in a picture	(see 'Form') Make close observational studies of the texture of natural and made objects	Extend the pattern work to integrate both shape and line	Consider the weight and balance of shapes in a picture	Model hollow and solid forms including surface quality and texture	Draw overlapping shapes of objects to create a sense of space	Discuss reasons why the artist made the work of art look the way it does
Hr's per yr:	5	5	5	5	5	5	5	5	5

Total number of hours per year-45

NB. Each 5 hours allocated to a visual element focus should include between 10% and 20% discussion/review time

NB. Some incorporation of previous years' learning should be encouraged within each visual element focus.

FIG 10.9

Art visual elements: Key Stage 2

© London Borough of Barking and Dagenham 1995

DURHAM GUIDELINES FOR THE IMPLEMENTATION OF ART IN THE NATIONAL CURRICULUM

SCHEME OF WORK

AREA OF EXPERIENCE: DRAWING	KEY STAGE I	Activities should bring together requirements from both ATs wherever possible.	
PROGRAMME OF STUDY	VISUAL ELEMENTS & TECHNIQUES	KNOWLEDGE & UNDERSTANDING	IDEAS FOR INVESTIGATING & MAKING
AT1 Investigating and Making Pupils should be taught to: a record what has been experienced, observed and imagined; b recognise images and artefacts as sources of ideas for their work; c select and sort images and artefacts, and use this source material as a basis for their work; experiment with tools and techniques for drawing, painting, printmaking, collage and sculpture, exploring a range of materials, including textiles; e experiment with visual elements, e.g. pattern, texture, colour, line, tone, shape, form, space, to make images and artefacts, using the range of media in d; f review what they have done and describe what they might change or develop in future work. AT2 Knowledge and Understanding Pupils should be taught to: a identify in the school and the locality the work of artists, craftspeople and designers; b recognise visual elements, e.g. pattern, texture, colour, line, tone, shape, form, space, in images and artefacts; c recognise differences and similarities in art, craft and design from different times and places; d respond to the ideas, methods or approaches used in different styles and traditions; c describe works of art, craft and design in simple terms, and explain what they think and feel about these. Materials for Drawing Different grades of pencil HB, 2B, 4B, 6B Coloured pencil, wax crayon, chalk pastel, oil pastel, charcoal, chalk, fixative, (hairspray) felt tip pen, ballpoint pen, rollerball pen, fine liner, marker pen, dip pen, ink Brushes — a range of sizes, hair and bristle Coloured and textured papers — different weights, sizes and shapes. Drawing board Computer-drawing programmes Magnifying glass, viewfinder, spotlight, filters, mirrors	Line Experiment with mark-making using different qualities of line. Unbroken line, making scribbles, free expressive lines, using outline. Varying the gap between lines, the thickness and pressure. Using a ruler for pattern work. Experiment with a variety of drawing materials and surfaces. Drawing with ink using soft fine brushes or pen nibs. Blowing ink with a straw. Drawing with wool, string etc. Tone Making dots, making marks, varying the gap, thickness and pressure, hatching, cross hatching. Spattering, spraying, stippling with ink Tonal contrasts — light, dark. Linear tone, blocked tone, simple blending. Depth and solidity of tone. Combining media Working on different coloured papers. Pattern and Texture Adding pattern to drawings — dots, stripes, checks etc. Match textures and patterns. Copy patterns and textures. Design and make patterns Rubbings of natural and made forms Use of a variety of tools and materials Drawing on a range of surfaces, e.g. textured papers, imprinting in clay Combining media Colour Experimenting with coloured drawing media Drawing using dots and lines of different colours. Hatching, cross hatching Mixing and blending with soft pastels. Blowing ink with a straw to mix colour Making patterns with colour Using different coloured papers. Combining media Shape, Form and Space Using an outline to define shape Drawing with wire and string Draw around objects Overlapping shapes to create new shapes Making spaces between shapes Simple perspective — changes in size and overlap of shapes Picture space	Line Look and talk about artists who have used line in their work e.g.: Paul Klee, Vincent van Gogh, Leonardo da Vinci, Modigliani Art and design from different periods & cultures — Greek vase decoration, Celtic ornament, Fashion magazines, newspapers, books, photographs Tone Look and talk about artists and designers who have used tone in their work e.g.: — L.S. Lowry, Caravaggio, Samuel Palmer, Rembrandt, Picasso, Bill Brandt, Bridget Riley, Kathe Kollwitz Black and white photographs, magazine and newspaper images. Pattern and Texture Look and talk about artists who have used pattern and texture in their work e.g.: — William Morris, Laura Ashley, Edouard Vuillard, Fernand Leger, Islamic, Celtic, Indian, Egyptian art Fabrics, wrapping papers, wallpapers, rugs, carpets, cushions. Colour Look and talk about artists who have used colour in their work: — Impressionists, Pointillists, Fauvists Gauguin, Cezanne, Titian, Mark Rothko, Frank Stella, Joan Eardley, David Hockney Magazine pictures, graphics, colour photographs, book illustrations. Shape, Form and Space Look and talk about artists and designers who have used shape, form & space in their work: — Henry Moore, Henri Matisse, Giacometti, Alexander Calder, Bernard Leach, Christo, Christopher Wren Book illustration, illuminated letters, photographs, graphics, artefacts	Line Making marks with a variety of materials Scribbling, doodling, working to music Drawing from observation — looking for lines in surroundings and everyday objects e.g. toys, shoes Compare drawings of the same thing made from memory. Collect and sort images/objects for line. Imaginary drawing — fantastic fashion, hairstyles/hair/body adornment — reference to other cultures. Tone Tonal pictures — using black, white and grey From observation draw subjects such as dandelion, dried flowers, shells, urchins, pebbles etc. Draw larger than life — use a magnifying glass. Use a spotlight to look for strong light and shadow. Collect and sort images/objects for tone Experiment with a range of materials and techniques including charcoal, chalk and soft pencils Pattern and Texture Look for patterns and textures in observed objects. Match textures using appropriate marks e.g. fur Make rubbings of different textures & patterns Collect and sort images/objects for pattern and texture. Make a scrapbook of different patterns to stimulate pattern drawing. Draw fabric and tile patterns Design wallpaper/wrapping paper/fabrics Colour Observational and expressive drawing using colour and mixed media. Recording colours of natural and made objects. Collect and sort for colour. Recording colours of the seasons, the weather. Exploring colours in mixed media Imaginative work: book covers and illustrations Use of colour in picture and pattern making Shape, Form and Space Body shapes, hands, feet, fingers. Shapes of objects, letters, words. Geometric shapes. Animal silhouettes. Decorated words and letters. Shape and form in structure and nature. Looking for shapes inside shapes. Exploring space in picture making

DURHAM GUIDELINES FOR THE IMPLEMENTATION OF ART IN THE NATIONAL CURRICULUM

SCHEME OF WORK

AREA OF EXPERIENCE:— DRAWING	KEY STAGE 2	Activities should bring together requirements from both ATs wherever possible.	
PROGRAMME OF STUDY	VISUAL ELEMENTS & TECHNIQUES	KNOWLEDGE & UNDERSTANDING	IDEAS FOR INVESTIGATING & MAKING
AT1 Investigating and Making Pupils should be taught to: a develop skills for recording from direct experience and imagination, and select and record from first-hand observation; b record observations and ideas, and collect visual evidence and information, using a sketchbook; experiment with ideas for their work suggested by visual and other source material; c experiment with and develop control of tools and techniques for drawing, painting, printmaking, collage and sculpture, exploring a range of materials, including textiles; d experiment with and use visual elements, e.g. *pattern, texture, colour, line, tone, shape, form and space*, to make images and artefacts for different purposes, using the range of media in d; e identify how visual elements, e.g. *pattern, texture, colour, line, tone, shape, form, space*, are used in images and artefacts for different purposes; f reflect on and adapt their work in the light of what they intended and consider what they might develop in future work. **AT2 Knowledge and Understanding** Pupils should be taught to: a identify in the school and the locality the materials and methods used by artists, craftspeople and designers; b recognise ways in which works of art, craft and design reflect the time and place in which they are made; c compare the ideas, methods or approaches used in different styles and traditions; d express ideas and opinions, developing an art, craft and design vocabulary, and the ability to use knowledge to support views. **Materials for Drawing** Different grades of pencil HB, 2B, 4B, 6B eraser, coloured pencil, wax crayon, chalk pastel, oil pastel, charcoal & chalk, conte crayon, fixative, (hairspray), felt pens, ballpoint pen, rollerball, marker, dip pen and ink brushes — a range of sizes — hair and bristle coloured and textured papers — different weights & sizes drawing board, sketchpad, tracing paper, computer — drawing programmes magnifying glass, viewfinder, spotlight, filters papers — convex, concave.	**Line** Experiment further with mark making developing greater control of drawing tools. Varying the sensitivity of line. Applying knowledge of descriptive and expressive qualities of line. Using line to show volume, depth or distance. Drawing geometric shapes and straight lines freehand. Making purposeful lines which describe form and space. Optical effects of line and distortion. Wax etching **Tone** Experiment with depth and solidity of tone. Applying dots and marks which show tonal contrasts, shadows and highlights. Spattering, stippling and spraying. Using hatching and cross hatching to indicate tone. Blending, smudging and shading with different media. Developing a tonal scale using dot, line and shade. Erasing and heightening tone. Using linear and blocked tone as appropriate. **Pattern and Texture** Experiment further with pattern and texture. Recreating pattern and texture seen in natural and made forms. Developing the use of pattern in drawings. Creating texture using different media and combinations. Use of scale — enlargements — use of magnifying glass. Patterns using repeated shapes. Tessellation, rotation, symmetry, brick repeat, full, half drop, mirror image, counter change. **Colour** Experiment further with colour. Using a wider range of coloured drawing media. Colour mixing and blending. With soft pastels Overlapping patches of colour, hatching & cross hatching. Matching colour to direct observations. Using different coloured papers. Applying colour expressively and imaginatively Using colour to convey feelings and emotions **Shape, Form and Space** Experiment further with shape, form and space. Use of light and shadow to indicate depth and volume. Combining visual elements to create form. Positive and negative shapes. Drawing from different viewpoints — above, below, sideview. Using an outline. Drawing with wire and string. Perspective. Picture space and composition.	**Line** Look and talk about artists who have used line in their work e.g.:— Henri Matisse, David Hockney, Quentin Blake, Gerald Scarfe, Paul Klee, Op Art, Art Nouveau, Aubrey Beardsley. Design & architecture, photographs, book illustrations, prints Magazine cuttings, advertisements **Tone** Look and talk about artists who have used tone in their work e.g.:— Pieter Bruegel, Robert Motherwell, Cubists, Georges Braque, Picasso, Rembrandt. Art, craft & design from different periods and cultures Black and white photographs, newspaper and magazine pictures **Pattern and Texture** Look and talk about artists who have used pattern and texture in their work e.g.: — Aubrey Beardsley, William Morris, Laura Ashley, Antoni Gaudi, Islamic, Celtic, Indian, Egyptian art. Design, Fashion, book covers and illustrations, pottery, fabrics, photographs, architecture **Colour** Look and talk about artists who have used colour in their work e.g.:— Oskar Kokoschka, Edvard Munch, Wassily Kandinsky, Franz Marc Impressionists, Expressionists, Fauvists. Folk art and design including costume, artefacts, textiles Colour photographs and magazine pictures, book illustrations, prints. **Shape, Form and Space** Look and talk about artists who have used shape, form & space in their work e.g.:— Paula Modersohn-Becker, Giacometti, Elizabeth Frink, Picasso. Art and design from different periods & cultures, including sculpture, monuments, architecture, photographs	**Line** Use the knowledge gained in drawing for a variety of purposes, using a variety of marks and materials Drawing from first hand observation — focus on linear qualities of natural and made forms. Investigative drawing. Use a sketchbook to develop ideas, to change and modify designs. Drawing from imagination — doodling; developing into considered designs in a variety of media **Tone** Tonal pictures — using black, white and a range of tones. Use a spotlight to enhance tonal contrasts. Work from black and white photographs — copied upside down. Extend half a picture by tonal drawing. Use a viewfinder for selective focusing. Use a magnifying glass for close observation. Observe and record reflective surfaces e.g. kettle, spoon, mirrors, machinery. Use a sketchbook. **Pattern and Texture** Patterns in structures and nature. Look at sections of a drawing for pattern. Make abstract pictures. Draw objects on a patterned tablecloth. Use rubbings for texture, backgrounds or collages. Develop control of rulers and compasses in pattern. Teach when to use tracing paper and stencils. Design a repeat pattern for a fabric Use of computer in design work. Use a sketchbook. **Colour** Observational and expressive drawing using colour and mixed media. Exploring colour association with moods; feelings, Imaginative work e.g. story illustration, imaginary landscape, atmospheric pictures. Drawing used to plan larger scale work. Prepare a range of colourways for design work using the computer as appropriate. Collect examples of colour, mix and match colours. Keep examples and experiments in sketchbook **Shape, Form and Space** Geometric shapes and natural forms. Illustrated letters, portrait profiles, trees, leaves, shells. Composition, simple perspective. Landscapes, interiors, showing background, middleground and foreground. Objects appearing smaller as they recede. Overlapping shapes. The use of a sketchbook to develop ideas.

FIG 10.10
Drawing: Key Stages 1 and 2

Assessment policy statement

Your general policy statement about assessment is best kept as simple as possible and with detail about its implementation and the methods to be used (e.g. examples of record cards, self-evaluation profiles) included in a number of appendices. A typical outline statement might be as follows:

> Children's work in art will be regularly assessed against National Curriculum Attainment Targets and will be reported to parents at the end of Key Stages 1 and 2 against the End of Key Stage Statements for Years 2 and 6.
>
> Pupils will keep examples of work across the Key Stage in order to assist in the assessment of their progress and achievement and will be encouraged to make personal assessments of their work. Some of these examples will be of such work, as in observational drawing and the use of the visual elements of art, that will be repeated each year in order to demonstrate pupil's progress.
>
> The art coordinator will maintain folders of examples of work in art for each year group in the school and these will be used to assist teaching staff in ensuring standardisation of assessment procedures for the subject.

You should be able to use the checklist in Part 3 as the framework for an outline statement of policy about the methods of assessment you will use in your own school.

The number of appendices you will need to include will depend upon how well assessment procedures are established in your school and how experienced your colleagues are in using them.

The following aspects of assessment might be included in these appendices.

What evidence you will use for the assessment of children's work

How annual progress will be recorded

How consistency of standards in assessment will be ensured

How you will involve children in the assessment of their progress

How you will report progress to parents at the end of key stages

What evidence will you use for the assessment of children's work?

This section will refer to the procedures for selecting and storing evidence of the work of individual pupils for assessment at the end of each year or at the end of the key stage. It will include reference to the use of such devices as drawing profiles to monitor children's progress and how sketchbooks will be used in the process of assessment.

How annual progress will be recorded

This section will include examples of any record cards in use in your school to record the work covered in each class and what pro forma you will use to record children's progress and achievements in art at the end of each year.

Look at the example below of a record card, modelled upon the End of Key Stage Statements that is used to record children's achievements at the end of each (Figure 11.1).

How consistency of standards in assessment will be ensured

This section will refer to any procedures you will use within the school to establish consistency of assessment standards between colleagues (e.g. through the regular sharing of and discussion about children's work), the subject coordinator's responsibilities for maintaining records and examples of children's work and the procedures for reviewing and moderating children's work at the end of key stages.

FIG 11.1
Pupil's record card

Name: Class:
Year: Teacher:

KS1 End of Key Stage Descriptions	Working Towards	Meeting	Exceeding
Recording ideas and feelings with confidence			
Developing ability to represent what is seen and touched			
Choosing resources and materials for their visual and tactile qualities to stimulate and develop ideas			
Working practically and imaginatively with materials, tools and techniques			
Presenting work in two dimensions			
Presenting work in three dimensions			
Describing and comparing images and artefacts in simple terms			
Recognising differences in methods and approaches used			
Making links with their own work			

© Falmer Press Ltd

How you will involve children in the assessment of their progress

This section will review the ways in which you will encourage children to review and appraise their own work including the use of any self-assessment profiles by children.

How you will report progress to parents at the end of key stages

This section will detail the arrangements for reporting to parents at the end of each key stage, the relationship between the format for reporting at the end of each year and that for reporting to parents, how you will use appropriate non-specialist language for reporting to parents.

You will find it useful to refer to the extract below from *Expectations in Art at Key Stages 1 and 2* (SCAA, 1997) which summarises what children should have achieved at the end of Years 2, 4 and 6 in each of the six Key Strands of the National Curriculum in art (see Figure 11.2).

SCAA (1997) *Expectations in Art at Key Stages 1 and 2*

ASPECTS	By the end of YEAR 2 the majority of children:	By the end of YEAR 4 the majority of children:	By the end of YEAR 6 the majority of children:
Record responses, including observations of the natural and made environment	record with confidence what they observe, experience and imagine	represent what they observe, experience and imagine	select and record from firsthand observation with some accuracy and attention to detail
Gather resources and materials, using them to stimulate and develop ideas	select, sort and use images and artefacts as source material for their work	collect visual evidence and information in a sketchbook and use as source material for their work	select and record visual and other information in a sketchbook and experiment with ideas suggested
Explore and use two- and three-dimensional media, working on a variety of scales	work practically and imaginatively with a range of media	explore and combine media and experiment with visual elements for different purposes	experiment with and control media and visual elements, selecting appropriately for different purposes
Review and modify their work as it progresses	review their work, describing what they might change or develop in future work	reflect on and adapt their work in the light of what they intended	identify ways in which their work can be developed and improved
Develop understanding of the work of artists, craftspeople and designers, applying knowledge to their own work	describe and compare works of art, craft and design in simple terms, recognising differences in method and approach	identify similarities and differences in method and approach, recognising how visual elements are used for different purposes	recognise ways in which works of art, craft and design reflect the time and place in which they are made
Respond to and evaluate art, craft and design, including their own and others' work	respond to ideas, methods or approaches, making links with their own work	compare ideas, methods or approaches including those used in different styles and traditions	evaluate their own and others' work in the light of what was intended

FIG 11.2
Summary of achievement at Key Stages 1 and 2

This section may also include reference to the use, and the display and presentation of children's work, as a means to inform parents, governors and visitors about the levels of achievement by children in their work in art and design in your school.

Chapter 12

Art policy on materials and resources

This section will outline the arrangements within your school for the organisation, distribution and use of tools and materials for your work in art and design and for the storage and use of such common visual resources as natural and made forms. The pattern will very much depend on the size of your school and how you distinguish between materials and resources which are common to all teaching bases (whether for class or year groups) and those which are centrally held for occasional use.

In most schools, the basic materials for drawing and painting and a range of papers and glues are kept in each class base and with more specialised materials, for example for work in textiles and ceramics, being held centrally. The following extract from the art policy for Thornbury Primary School, Plymouth is a typical general statement about the use and distribution of materials and visual resources.

All art areas are serviced with basic art materials for drawing painting, textiles and printmaking

All specialist resources are held centrally such as batik, screen print, ceramics, cartridge paper and extra textiles resources

All bases should be organised with a range of glues and papers

A range of papers is stored in the Infant area

All visual resources are held with the art coordinator and there is a wide provision of reproductions, postcards, books and posters

All artefacts are held in the Upper Junior base

There is a range of lengths of material for display purposes stored in colour banks in the pottery

The use and care of materials: health and safety

The section on materials and resources should include a brief statement about the need to encourage the careful and sensible use of tools materials at all times, both in the interests of economy and to satisfy the requirements of the 'Health and Safety at Work Act':

 Children will be taught the safe and sensible use of all tools and materials used in art and will be made aware of any risks associated with the use of particular tools and materials, e.g. scissors and cutting knives, using jantings and hot wax in making a batik etc.

In some schools, the art policy will include appendices dealing with the correct use of particular materials and processes as guidance for colleagues, see Figure 12.1, which details the organisation of the use of materials in painting.

You will need to decide where you need to provide such detailed advice within your own art policy.

Visual resource and reference materials

The National Curriculum emphasises the importance of critical studies, therefore the resources section of your policy may need to refer to the visual materials you will require to support this work.

Refer back to pp. 75–7 for work in critical studies to remind yourself of the range of resources you can use in association with this work.

In your general policy statement about the use of resources for critical studies it will be sufficient to make the following general points:

FIG 12.1
Organisation of painting lessons

Organisation for painting lessons

A set of colours should include: 2 reds – vermilion
                                                     crimson
                                       2 blues – ultramarine
                                                       turquoise
                                       yellow – lemon
                                       white
                                       black

There should be water for mixing colours and water for cleaning brushes. A dirty brush should not be put into a clean colour — white should stay white! Some small plastic spoons for transferring paint to the palette is also useful.

Every child should have a mixing palette of some description.

A range of brushes should always be available and the children encouraged to select the most appropriate brush for each part of the painting.

        – a large brush for large areas
        – a small brush for more restricted areas
        – a fine, pointed brush for detail

The range of brushes available in school includes:

        – household brushes for murals, large
           paintings, etc.
        – long-handled hog hair brushes, round
           and flat headed in different sizes
        – short-handled brushes, sable or squirrel
           hair in different sizes

Care of equipment

From reception onwards children should be told *not* to use painting brushes for glue and not to leave brushes standing in paint or water for any length of time. Cleaning of equipment should become an integral part of the art lesson.

Children will have access to the work of artists, craftworkers and designers from different times and cultures through the school's collections of texts, posters, reproductions and photographs of artists' work.

Reference to and use will be made, of evidence of artists' and designers' work within the environment of the school and the local community.

Artists and designers working in the community will be encouraged to visit the school to talk about their own work.

Wherever possible, children will be given opportunities to see artists' and designers' work at first hand, through visits to local museums and galleries.

Coordinating, listing and cataloguing reference materials

If you teach in a large school, it may be necessary to include as an appendix, a list for reference of those artists' works which are represented in your school's collections. In some schools, the outline schemes of work include reference to those artists to be studied and evidence of whose work is available within the school. Where you have a common pattern of teaching themes working throughout your school from year to year, it will be helpful to collate a list of reference materials relevant to each of these themes.

It would also be useful to include a list of interesting examples of artists' and designers' work that can be found within the locality e.g. interesting buildings, examples of street furniture, artefacts, public art and murals, graphic design, local craft workshops etc.

The guiding principle should be to make it as simple as possible for colleagues to find and use reference materials to the work of artists and designers that will support their work in critical studies and other curriculum areas.

Display

If there already exists in your school a well-established tradition of using the display and presentation of children's work to celebrate achievement and enhance the environment of the school, your policy statement about display need consist only of a general summary of its several purposes, for example:

---

to celebrate the achievements of all children;
to improve the quality of the environment of the school;
to indicate standards of achievement, values and high expectations;
to inform parents, governors and visitors to the school about the range, nature and quality of work in art and design;
to support teaching and learning in art;
to encourage children's care and respect for each other's work.

Supporting appendices may be needed to provide colleagues with specific guidance about the different ways that display can be used, while some schools might include more detailed guidelines about how children's work will be mounted, displayed and presented. Where there are agreed procedures for the display of work you will need to establish consistent standards in the display and presentation of the children's work in classrooms and public areas of the school.

Special needs and differentiation

The policy documents for all schools will include details of policies for equal opportunities and special needs across all subject teaching and it will not always be necessary to refer specifically to special needs and differentiation in work in art and design. It might be useful to refer back to Chapter 8 and see whether any of these considerations require a specific mention in your policy. Otherwise it may be sufficient to include such a general statement as follows:

> *In art and design teaching, differentiation is based upon outcome, upon the response of individual children to a common task. Where children do have special needs because of disadvantage or special ability, it may be necessary occasionally, to differentiate by task to support the disadvantaged or to challenge the more able.*

Mention may also be made of the practice of using reference material relating to the work of artists and designers from a wide range of cultural backgrounds, both European and non-European, and to giving value to the work of women artists and designers.

Policies for using external agencies

If you have established a regular pattern of working with other institutions, agencies and individuals outside your school in support of your work in art and design, it will be sensible to record this in your art policy as a general statement of your intent to use whatever external resources will benefit your work.

You should include examples of such cooperation and it would be helpful to colleagues to list the names and addresses of helpful contacts as an appendix.

Examples might include some of the following:

- Members of the Local Advisory or Curriculum Support Service who work regularly with the school;
- The head of art and design department at your local secondary school where you share such initiatives as joint inservice workshops, exhibitions of pupils' work or practical workshops for pupils based either in your school, at the secondary school (such initiatives are quite common as part of the process of the transfer of pupils);
- Education officers at local museums or galleries;
- Artists, craftworkers and designers in the community who are willing to share their work with the school or allow visits to their studios/workshops;
- Commercial galleries or craft centres that welcome pupils as visitors to see the work in their collections;
- Officers at Regional Arts Associations, where they have a policy of providing supportive funding to schools for arts events.

Part four | Monitoring for quality

Chapter 13
Monitoring children's
achievement and progress in art

Chapter 14
Strategies for monitoring and
recording progress in art

Chapter 13   Monitoring children's achievement and progress in art

This section deals with all those different aspects of teaching art which contribute to the way in which you and your colleagues make judgments about children's progress and achievements in making their work in art.

Many primary school teachers are diffident when it comes to judging children's art, often because they are not convinced of the need to do so. Prior to the National Curriculum there was no real requirement to assess pupils' progress in art, so most teachers have had little experience in making such judgments.

The National Curriculum also requires that children should be taught how to make their own judgments about their own art and that of other artists. It is expected that they will be given opportunities to reflect upon and review their own work and to evaluate the work of other artists, craftworkers and designers.

Your main task as coordinator will be to support your colleagues through putting in place some effective and simple procedures for appraising children's work in art.

It will also be essential for you to establish a strong link in working practice between **your monitoring and making judgments about children's progress and achievements in art** and the way in which you build into your work with children **opportunities for their reflecting upon their own work and making judgments about the work of others.**

This interplay between reflection upon their own work by pupils and appraisal by the teacher is fundamental to the effective monitoring of children's progress in making art. It also helps to make appraisal and reflection a natural part of the working process in art.

Reflection and appraisal in the National Curriculum

In the National Curriculum, the two Key Strands and Programmes of Study concerned with reflection and appraisal are described as follows:

In Attainment Target 1
Investigating and Making
Pupils should

Review and modify their work as it progresses

KS1
Review what they have done and describe what they might change or develop in future work

KS2
Reflect on and adapt their work in the light of what they intended and consider what they might develop in future work

In Attainment Target 2
Knowledge and Understanding
Pupils should

Respond to and evaluate art, craft and design, including their own and others' work

KS1
Respond to the ideas, methods or approaches used in different styles and traditions

Describe works of art, craft and design in simple terms and explain what they think or feel about them

KS2
Compare the ideas methods or approaches used in different styles and traditions

Express ideas and opinions, developing an art, craft and design vocabulary, and the ability to use knowledge to support their views.

These Programmes of Study reinforce those links between between knowing about art and making art that are inherent in its nature and long pattern of development within our culture.

Art progresses, develops and changes as artists bring to it their own experiences, their understanding, response and reaction to the work of others.

In teaching art to children in schools, you can help them to appraise their own work more effectively through linking discussion and review about their work to the study and appraisal of the work of other artists who have explored similar experiences and ideas.

Monitoring and appraising children's work in art

When starting to review your own school's policy for monitoring and appraising children's work in art it would be useful to begin by looking at those different teaching strategies and systems that support effective assessment and noting those in current practice in your own school.

Review which of these strategies are in common use by you and your colleagues in your school

 1 Talking with individual children about the work they are in progress of making
 2 Group discussion with children about work they have made at the end of a project
 3 Group discussion with children about the work of artists and designers
 4 Children using sketchbooks to make notes about, or comment upon, the work they are making
 5 Children writing about their own work
 6 Children writing about the work of other artists
 7 Children making work for 'drawing profiles'
 8 Teachers sharing children's work with each other to monitor progress and achievement
 9 Teachers using examples of children's work to identify criteria for assesement
10 Children completing self-assessment profiles about work they have made
11 Teachers completing assessment profiles about children's work
12 Teachers writing/reporting about children's work

These different strategies can be used in various combinations:
- to develop and support children's progress in coming to a better understanding of the work they have made, how they have made it, what ideas the work expresses and how their work relates to the work of other artists;
- to support children's review of their work and progress and to make decisions about developing future work;
- to help teachers to understand and identify how children progress in making different forms of art;
- to help teachers appraise children's work and to develop agreed criteria for making that appraisal.

Monitoring progression

The stages that children go through in making art as they progress through the primary school and the different kinds of work that they will make have already been outlined in Part 2 and these descriptions will help you in planning your schemes of work in art and should give you some guidance as to the context within which to set appropriate tasks in art for children in Key Stages 1 and 2.

It will be useful to begin to collect, systematically, examples of children's work from your own school to illustrate how progression takes place in the way that children represent and record familiar experiences and ideas. These will help you and your colleagues identify how children progress through these stages and how their work in art within the class group fits into the overall pattern.

Your collection could include half a dozen examples of children's work from each year group based on such familiar themes as follows:

from observation
self portrait
a spring plant
my shoe
view from my window

from memory/imagination
my favourite person
a family outing
my favourite meal

It will also be helpful to have collections of children's work from different year groups made in response to the same drawing or painting by another artist.

Such collections of work from different year groups will provide useful material for discussing progression in all aspects of your school's artwork.

Drawing profiles

In some schools, teachers have made a virtue of this reference to common subject matter throughout a school to develop the use of drawing profiles. (See Figure 13.1.)

Example of a drawing profile in use in one school

ART PROFILE

Name _____   D. O. B _____

Year Group _____   Teacher _____

Autumn Term   'My Mum' from memory
Spring Term   'A Plant' from observation
Summer Term   'An illustration for a favourite story' from imagination

This art profile form is to be included in the pupil's record folder. Each year pupils will produce three drawings so that progress can be monitored.

FIG 13.1
Art profile

© Falmer Press Ltd

This use of the common drawing task across a school to keep occasional track of developments from Key Stage 1 to Key Stage 2, has two useful functions: the drawings can be used as a basis for staff review and discussion about progression and they can also be retained to build up a personal drawing profile for individual children to record their progress through the school.

Some schools are now setting their pupils a common drawing task in each term, for example, asking all the children to make a drawing from observation in the autumn term, one from memory in the spring term and an imaginative drawing in the summer term. In these schools, each child will have a drawing profile of eighteen drawings made at regular intervals by the time they reach the end of Key Stage 2 and these will be a very useful record of their progress and development in one key aspect of their work in art and design.

Monitoring and matching progression

It is self-evident that children will progress naturally enough through the development stages of perception and that their drawings and paintings will mature and progress as they themselves mature and have regular practise in making images. Even in those schools where there is little by way of the structured teaching of art taking place such progression can be observed! However, you and your colleagues can support and encourage that progression by seeking ways to match the tasks that you set the children to their developmental stages.

Differentiated tasks

In planning to monitor the development of children's work through your own school, as in the use of drawing profiles, you should also consider how you can differentiate between the drawing tasks set to match the development and progress that children make in their work from Key Stage 1 to Key Stage 2.

Just as you set the children increasingly complex tasks in their work in language and in other subjects, you can similarly set them increasingly demanding tasks in their work in art and design by requiring them to make familiar images within increasingly demanding and challenging contexts.

For example, if you and your colleagues decide to use the figure as the starting point for a common drawing task you could consider placing the tasks within a different context in each Key Stage to allow for the developing abilities of the children in order that the tasks become more demanding with the context of the drawing of the figure. For example:

Key Stage 1
Draw a particular person
(*mother, friend, self*)
Draw someone dressed for a particular occasion
(*for a party, to go swimming, to go out in the rain*)

Key Stage 2
Draw yourself in a particular mood
(*feeling happy, looking puzzled*)
Draw a group of people showing their relative sizes
(*a family group, a bus queue*)
Draw yourself engaged in favourite activity
(*playing a game with a friend, opening a present, trying on a new outfit*)

Similarly, you can take any of those familiar artists you use in your work in critical studies and consider in what contexts you might ask children to respond to that work in order to ensure that progression is taking place in the level at which they are being asked to respond to that work.

Vincent Van Gogh is the most familiar of all artists whose work is studied and used in primary schools. All too often, children are asked to make work in response to his work in the same kind of way, irrespective of their age and level of maturity.

Look at the following six tasks that might be undertaken in reponse to his work and place them in order of complexity. Which would be most suitable to use in Key Stage 1, which in Key Stage 2?

Make a painting of sunflowers like those in Van Gogh's paintings

Make a study the different yellows, oranges, reds and browns that Van Gogh has used in one of his paintings of Sunflowers

Make studies of some of Van Gogh's drawings of trees made at different times to show how his style of drawing changed during his working life

Make a detailed study of part of one of Van Gogh's landscape paintings to show how he applied paint and used a swirling pattern of brushstrokes in his work

Make a painting of your own bedroom in the same style as that used by Van Gogh in his painting of his bedroom at Arles

Make comparative studies of drawings of peasants working made by Van Gogh and and those made by Jean-Francois Millet. What did Van Gogh learn about drawing from Millet?

Matching tasks to development stages: building progression into planning

These are just a few examples of ways in which you can match the monitoring of children's progress in making art to the kind of tasks you set them. There is a significant link between how well children progress and the way that you and your colleagues allow for this and build such opportunities for progression into your planning for different kinds of work.

The same principle applies to all aspects of your work in art with children. You can only monitor children's work effectively if you have built progression into your planning in such a way that your colleagues have a reasonably clear picture of what they can expect children to learn and achieve as they progress through the school. Chapter 9 deals with this in some detail.

It is sufficient here to give one example of the way in which an art coordinator has set out their general expectations for the children's progression and development in the use of drawing in their school. This outline provides a useful framework that teachers in this school can use when planning work with their class and gives them some understanding of how their teaching of drawing fits into the overall pattern within the school.

They can also use this framework as the basis for monitoring what kind of progress children are making in drawing, because the expectations for progress and development in drawing have been established for them.

Example of documenting progression
from school's art policy
Chaddlewood Primary School, Plympton

Drawing

Years 1/2	Years 3/4	Years 5/6
Scribbling, making marks and patterns freely	More emphasis on drawing from direct observation	Cotinuing to investigate and communiucate ideas through observed and expressive work
Drawing to tell a story — everyday things, self, family, pets, possessions	Drawing in a variety of ways and for different purposes. e.g. describing, analysing, inventing, expressing	Wide use of resources is necessary for a variety of starting points — including works of art from different times and cultures
Using symbols and shapes freely	Use of range of natural, made and environmental forms. …alongside good quality photographs and reproductions of works of art (other artists' drawings)	Children to collect and bring own resources to school and keep and use notebooks or sketchbooks
'Careful looking' drawings of familiar objects — collected and on display		
Use of soft pencils, chalk charcoal, pastels and . appropriately coloured paper	Encourage close looking and use of words about size, shape texture, tone etc, so that children learn to use all their senses in observing	Use wide range of media for drawing. Children choose materials appropriate to the task
Introduce view finders, peep holes and magnifying glasses		Encourage more subtle and complex use of art vocabulary
Thick, thin, pale and dark lines	Discuss technical problems when relevant to the task in hand	More demanding drawing tasks to encourage exploration of form and space e.g. drawing from several points of view, explaining overlapping and distance
Compare light/dark shiny/dull, pattened/plain, curved/straight etc.	Introduce use of mixed media — using combinations of materials to make a drawing	
Use language to focus on detail	Discuss appropriateness of materials used	

Developing children's evaluation of their own work

In working with children in making art, in making judgments about their work and in encouraging them to make their own judgments, you do have one very significant advantage compared with working in many other subjects. Making art is a visual process and because you can see and share with the children what they are doing, it is comparatively easy to enter into dialogue with them about what is happening, about how they are making their work and how their ideas are emerging.

In good practice, children's appraisal of their own work should grow and develop naturally from their early descriptions and comments about their story-telling drawings towards a more considered and searching dialogue about the quality of their making and the range of ideas they explore.

In art, evaluation is rooted in that structured dialogue with children about their making and where assessment and appraisal are continuously negotiated between teacher and taught.

Individual questioning and discussion

Although talk and discussion about making art is a natural part of the way that you and your colleagues work in art with young children in your school, how efficiently is such sharing of work used and developed so that the dialogue becomes constructive in helping the children to understand and appraise what they have achieved?

The following example is of the kind of questions that might be used by a teacher to generate dialogue and to support and extend that familiar task of making of a painting of a spring plant and its appraisal.

Focusing and looking questions
How is the plant going to fit onto the page?
Where are the stems thickest and thinnest?
Do some stems cross the others?
How many leaves are there on each stem?
Where are the biggest leaves?
How are the flower heads different from each other?
Do some have more petals than others?

Making questions
How many different colours can you see in the stem?
Where are the colours lightest and darkest?
How will you make these colours?
Which part of the plant will you need to paint first?
Where will you need to use the paint thickly?
How many different sizes of brush will your need?
What colours will you need to paint the flower heads?

Questions to encourage self evaluation
Stop and compare your painting with the plant you are looking at.
Are you sure that that colour is the right one to use?
Which part of the plant do you need to do more work on?
Which part of the painting are you most pleased with — why?

> Which was the most difficult thing to do in this painting?
> Would you make the painting differently if you had to do it again?
> What have you learnt that is new to you in making this painting?
>
> **In consulatation with your colleagues, can you construct similar sets of questions that would generate dialogue for other kinds of tasks?**
>
> e.g.   making a clay figure of an animal
>   designing and making a weaving of a landscape
>   making a drawing of a view from the window

The key factor in constructing these kind of dialogues is for the questioning to be specific to the task and to different stages of the task so that in responding the child is required to consider some particular aspect of the act of making.

Structured group discussion

Although individual negotiation between teacher and child will be the dominant method for encouraging children to consider and appraise their making in art, you will also need to consider ways in which you can encourage colleagues to use group discussion and sharing as another vehicle for self-evaluation.

It will be useful to review with colleagues their use of group discussion and which of the different forms it can take that are appropriate for particular purposes.

Peer group discussion (in small groups)	This is particularly useful in the early stages of an art project where children can share with each other their ideas about the task:
	talking with each other about the colours and shapes they can see in a group of objects set before them;
	talking with each other about the ideas generated by comparing reproductions of different works of art.
Reviewing work in progress	Where children may discuss and compare in small groups the preliminary studies and drawings they have in preparation for making work and compare their different ideas for taking this work forward
	Sharing and appraisal of work. Recognition of work made by children does take place in school assemblies and this is an appropriate way to celebrate particular achievements.
End of session review	Where the teacher leads a five minute discussion at the end of the art session to generate talk about what has been achieved and learnt in that session

End of project review	Where the teacher coordinates group discussion in association with the display and presentation of the finished work from a project. With older children this can be used as a framework for the children writing about their achievements or completing self-assessment profiles about their work.

Art language

In order to be able talk and write about their own work and that of other artists, and to reflect upon their own achievements, children will need to learn and to use an appropriate art vocabulary. Art and design, like all disciplines, has its own vocabulary of terms that are used to name and describe specific tools, methods and processes, different kinds of work and, most importantly, different qualities of visual appearance.

The beginnings of an art vocabulary will emerge naturally enough where there is a consistent use of good structured talk about the work in progress — for example where children are asked to talk specifically about the way in which they mix and match colours, to use the proper names for colours as in distinguishing between a vermilion (orange red) and a crimson (blue red).

Similarly, their art vocabulary will develop when they are asked to talk and write about the work of different artists and different forms of art and begin to know the difference between forms of art such as a portrait and a self portrait, processes such as carving, screen printing and water colour paintings, and different kinds of art such as abstract, impressionist and symbolic.

You may find it useful to construct a check list of an art or critical vocabulary for inclusion in your art policy to guide colleagues. Such check lists are best organised in groups of words dealing with different aspects of art.

Here are some examples you can extend and build upon:

Colour	Materials and methods	What kind of art
cold	mural	abstract
dull	etching	representational
tint	lino print	post-impressionist
translucent	sketch	cubist
opaque	pastel	classical

Writing about art

Although there is some reluctance on the part of many teachers to ask children to write about their work in art — most frequently because they doubt the value of children writing about something that can be better expressed in the making of the art work — there are many occasions when writing about what they have made and why and how they have made it will give children a more structured opportunity to consider and reflect upon what they achieved.

It can also be argued that as most children are motivated by and enthusiatic about their work in art and are interested in the work of other artists, that this in itself is suffucient motivation for the writing.

Consider the following list of writing activities and review which of them are commonly in use in your school and which might usefully support children's appraisal of their own making.

Making notes of such technical processes as mixing colour or making a coil pot

Describing how a work was made, using a combination of text and diagrams

Describing how another artist has made a work

Reviewing the progress of their work from preliminary studies through to completion

'Brain-storming' in small groups their response to the work of another artist

Writing about work they like and dislike, justifying their preferences

Comparing work by different artists working to a common theme

Writing about their visits to galleries and museums

Self-assessment profiles

There is value in encouraging children to write about their own work and their achievements in art. It can also be very useful to use children's written comments and evaluations of their own work as part of the process of monitoring and appraising their progress. Many schools adopt this approach, particularly in Key Stage 2, when children comment on their own work at the end of each major project, or make notes in their sketchbooks.

It can be useful to formalise these personal and written comments to provide a framework or self-assessment profile within which such comments might be made at, for example, termly intervals. Some children find it easier to make their comments and order their responses within the framwork of a self-assessment profile.

The example shown below comes from a school where children are asked to describe and comment upon their work in Key Stage 1 within the following simple framework (Figure 13.2):

Pupil self evaluation profile: Key Stage 1

Name	Class	Date
Task		
Research		
What I did		
The things I liked		
How I could have made it better		

FIG 13.2
Pupil self-evaluation profile: Key Stage 1

© Falmer Press Ltd

Working with older children, from Year 4 onwards, the questions used to form a self-assessment profile would need to be more demanding, in tune with their growing maturity.

Consider the self-evaluation profile for older children below, compare it with the previous one and review with colleagues how appropriate it might be to use such profiles in your own work and, how they might be ammended for use in your own school and how frequently they should be used (Figure 13.3).

Pupil self-evaluation profile: Key Stage 2

Name	Class	Date
What resources or references did you start with?		
How did you make your drawings and studies? What materials and techniques did you use?		
Explain what choices and changes you made as the work progressed		
What other artists' work did you refer to? Did you find some of their ideas and methods helpful?		
Comment on your final piece of work. What improvements could be made to it?		
Has this given ideas for further work you would like to do?		

FIG 13.3
Pupil self-evaluation profile: Key Stage 2

© Falmer Press Ltd

Chapter 14

Strategies for monitoring and recording progress in art

Your school will have an overall policy for the regular monitoring and recording of children's progress in all subjects. The way in which you structure the monitoring of children's work in art will be determined to some extent by this policy, as for example in the frequency of assessment points and in the agreed form of reporting to parents.

You and your colleagues will also need to consider how to put in place and use some of those strategies for monitoring children's progress in art that are specific to the subject itself.

Reviewing children's work with colleagues

Because your colleagues will bring to their work in art a variety of levels of experience and contrasting attitudes to the subject, it will be particularly important to support them through regular review and discussion about the progress and development of children's work.

Teachers need to know at what level their pupils can work in different aspects of art and should, in addition, have some sense of how the level of work in their year group relates to pupils' work in the year above and below them. Without this knowledge, most primary school teachers will find it difficult to make reasonable assessments of the quality of work the children are currently making.

There has already been considerable discussion in this chapter about ways of identifying and recording children's progress in making art and some of these, like the development and use of drawing profiles, will provide a very useful basis for discussion and review with individuals or with groups of colleagues about what is happening in their class or year group.

Obviously enough, your responsibilities as art coordinator will require you to find effective ways to do this, either through the tactful negotiation with individual teachers or through such strategies as chairing/leading discussion with teachers in a year group or Key Stage to review their pupils' response to a drawing profile task.

The procedures for constructing and using descriptions of achievement for children's work in art are dealt with in detail in the section on reporting.

The display and presentation of children's achievements in art

As it is more than likely that your responsibilities as coordinator include oversight of the display and presentation of children's work throughout the school, you can also seek ways to use the presentation of children's work as a means to inform colleagues about both levels of achievement and progression within the subject.

There is considerable virtue in using the display of children's work didactically to inform the onlooker about what has happened in the process of making a work, as well as to celebrate the children's achievements.

To do this, a display of children's work from a project should include the following:

- the source material used to generate the work; e.g. collections of objects, photographs, reproductions of artists' work;

- the preliminary drawings and notes made by the children to investigate ideas about the starting points and resources;

- finished work by a number of children to illustrate the range of achievement;

- any explanatory notes that might be needed to illuminate the work;

- comments by the children about what they have achieved.

Where such didactic display of children's work is used publicly and within individual classrooms it will do much to generate informed discussion about the work both by children and by colleagues. It can also usefully inform parents, visitors and governors about the nature and purpose of the work that you and your colleagues are undertaking in your school.

Working to common themes

There are occasions when it will be appropriate for all the children in the school to be asked to work to a common theme in art, as generally happens in all schools at Christmas and where other occasions or seasons lend themselves to such venture. For example, in 1990, nearly every child in every school in the country made a work based on one of Van Gogh's paintings in celebration of the centenary of his death!

The presentation of children's work in response to such occasions can be very useful in that they provide an instant visual map of the way that certain kinds of images are made by children at different stages in their development, and this can serve as a useful basis for staff discussion.

In some schools, the occasional use of such common themes is negotiated by the coordinator for the purpose of supporting good staff development and in pursuit of extending the teachers' knowledge and understanding of how progression takes place.

The illustrations (Figures 14.1, 14.2, 14.3, 14.4) are from an exhibition of children's work from Reception to Year 3 at Stoke Hill First School in Exeter, where the work across the school was based upon the figure and the coordinator negotiated with teachers in each year group about the context within which they should introduce the figure with their class. The work by all the children in the school was displayed in the school hall.

FIG 14.1
Reception: Portrait of a woman: fibre tip pen

FIG 14.2
Yr 1: My friend: tempera

FIG 14.3
Yr 2: Child in costume: crayon and pastel

FIG 14.4
Yr 3: Seated couple: pencil and charcoal

Suggestion

Review what strategies you might use to encourage colleagues towards the consistent use of sketchbooks from year to year.

Using sketchbooks to monitor and identify progression

The use of sketchbooks and their differing purposes has already been discussed pp. 71–2.

Where sketchbooks are used and developed consistently, they can be very useful evidence in monitoring children's progress. They will record not only the child's progress in their drawing over a period of time, but also the development of their ideas and thinking. When children are encouraged to use them to record their ideas about work and to include resource material, that has generated their ideas for work and their comments upon their making.

The standard A4 sketchbook in use in most primary schools is easily storable and transferable with the children from class to class. It is valuable to the teacher at the beginning of a new academic year to be able to flick through a child's sketchbook, both to key quickly into the level at which that child is working and to open up discussion with the child about previous work which might be developed and built upon in coming year.

It will also be possible to include in sketchbooks examples or photcopies of some finished work which will be additionally useful towards appraising children's work, particularly at the end of each key stage.

Teacher assessment profiles

Although there has been considerable emphasis here upon developing systems for monitoring children's progress in art through the use of self-assessment profiles and other associated strategies, there will also be a need to develop and use in your school an agreed system whereby teachers record their own assessments of their children's work in art. These will serve as the basis for reporting to parents annually, as well as for the end of key stage reporting.

You will need to give careful thought as to the most effective way to report on children's progress and achievements in art to their parents. How you go about this will largely be determined by the assessment policies present in your own school and the form of reporting that has been set in place in response to the demands of the National Curriculum that parents should be better informed about their children's progress and should receive written statements about their progress at the end of each key stage.

Many schools and some LEAs have already put in place teacher assessment profiles for use in recording and monitoring children's progress in art, many of which are based, logically enough, on the pattern of Key Strands and Programmes of Study for the subject in the National Curriculum. One such example is illustrated in Figure 14.5.

Although this profile accurately reflects the National Curriculum requirements for the subject, many teachers might find it somewhat cumbersome to use in its detail. You will need to put in place an assessment profile that is acceptable to all your colleagues and which they can use with confidence and understanding. It is worth looking at several different models in use in other schools and discussing these with colleagues before you seek to implement this kind of reporting.

For example: compare the structure of the assessment profile (Figure 14.5) with the simpler one in Figure 14.6 and review with colleagues how you might use these two models as the basis for negotiating an acceptable assessment profile for use in your own school.

Reporting achievement

As the end of Key Stage Statements for art are no more than an objective description of what experiences should be covered in each key stage, they only tell us what the child has done and give no indication as to the level of quality at which the child has worked in the various aspects of the art and design curriculum.

If you are to inform parents about their children's progress and development in art, together with colleagues in your school,

Example of assessment profile (1) based upon the Key Strands for art

Art and Design Annual Assessment	Key Stage	
Name	Teacher	
Assessment criteria	Comments	Date
Recording from experience, observation and imagination		
Exploring materials, tools and techniques		
Using the visual language of art *line, tone, colour, pattern, texture, shape, form and space*		
Talking about work and describing how it might be changed or developed		
Awareness of art, craft and design in the school and locality		
Ability to recognise visual elements in images and artefacts		
Knowledge of art from different times and cultures		
Response to ideas and methods used in different styles and traditions		
Ability to describe works of art and to make judgments about them		

FIG 14.5   © Falmer Press Ltd
Assessment profile based on Key Strands for art

Example of assessment profile (2) based upon a simplification of the Key Strands for art

Key Stage	Year	
Name	Age	Date

AT1
Investigating:
through drawing from experience, memory and imagination
developing ideas for making work from different resources

Making:
using tools, materials and methods
understanding and using the visual elements of art

Reviewing:
appraising own work

AT2
Using knowledge of other artists' work to develop their own ideas

Knowing about and understanding other artists' work from a variety of times and cultures

FIG 14.6   © Falmer Press Ltd
A simplified assessment profile

you will need to develop **criteria** by which you can assess children's work.

This section is therefore concerned with identifying both the criteria by which you can assess children's work in art and how such criteria might relate to their development and progression through different stages in their work.

Developing criteria to monitor and assess children's progress in art

In art, it is not as appropriate, as in some other subjects, to assess children's progress in terms of subject content — by asking, 'what have they learnt about?'. Work in art and design is not content specific to a particular age or year group. Making a self portrait or a landscape painting are activities that are equally appropriate at different stages in the artist's life whether undertaken by a child of five or by an artist in maturity. **Differentiation** in art and design has always been achieved by **assessing the level of quality at which children and students respond to a common task**.

This will mean, that at the end of Key Stages 1 and 2, you will need to be able to describe at what level of quality a child is recording familiar made and natural forms or how well they are handling and using the visual elements of art such as colour, shape, pattern etc. In order to do this you will need to become familiar with those criteria that describe achievement in specific experiences within art and design.

Within your school, you will need to share and review children's work with your colleagues in order to begin to identify what are modest, average or significant achievements by children in different aspects of their work in art and design.

The Schools Curriculum and Assessment Authority refer to these three levels of achievement as:

working towards expectation for the key stage
working at
working beyond

You will obviously be appraising a body of work by each child at the end of each key stage and your assessment will be informed through knowing about how their work has developed and changed over a period of time and as they move from year to year.

You can usefully refer to the OFSTED Report on their first tranche of inspections of work in art in a cross section of primary schools to see what expectations the OFSTED Inspectors have of children's achievements in art at the end of each key stage. (*Art: A Review of Inspection Findings 1993/1994*, HMSO, 1995) These 'Benchmarks' of knowledge, understanding and skills describe the OFSTED expectations of what children should have achieved by the end of Years 2, 4 and 6 in key areas of work in the National Curriculum.

Use these benchmark statements (Figure 14.7) to review with colleagues how progression is taking place from Key Stage 1 to Key Stage 2 and how you can begin to identify and report upon children's progress and achievements in art.

You will find below some samples of end of key stage descriptions of achievement which were written by a group of teachers from the London Borough of Barking and Dagenham who looked at different kinds of children's work in conjunction with using the OFSTED benchmark descriptions in order to produce examples of descriptions of different levels of achievement in art.

Use these examples (Figure 14.8) as the basis for discussion with colleagues about the levels of achievement in art by children in your own school and how you might report upon them.

Such school-based inservice activities are very valuable in order to help colleagues become more experienced and confident in making judgments about children's work and in reporting upon their achievements.

They can provide the focus for teachers to become more familiar with the practice of sharing and moderating children's work and thus becoming more experienced and skilled in 'reading' what is happening and being achieved in different kinds of art and design activities.

End of Key Stage Statements: OFSTED 'Benchmarks'

Using the visual elements of art	
Year 2	Pupils can show their awareness of the visual elements (line, tone, colour, pattern. shape, form and space) through practical activities.
Year 4	They can show their knowledge and understanding of the visual elements of art through continued practical activity.
Year 6	Pupils can show their knowledge of the visual elements through practical exploration and will have begun to develop some elements of a personal style of expression.
Investigating and using resources	
Year 2	They have direct experience of collecting, sorting, handling and talking about natural and made things and visual images. These stimuli encourage them to communicate personal ideas about what they have seen, remembered or imagined in visual form.
Year 4	They can gather and organise ideas, including the use of sketchbooks, within a theme and can begin to plan their work in stages. They begin to distinguish between the different functions of drawing.
Year 6	They can use a sketchbook to record observations and ideas related to a specific theme and are able, with guidance, to use these in support of their work. They can distinguish between the different functions of drawing and use them selectively.
Making	
Year 2	Their knowledge of art is extended by experimenting with and demonstrating increasing skill in using a range of media and tools and techniques through drawing, painting, modelling, printmaking, collage, textile and clay work.
Year 4	Through a steady growth in manual dexterity, they are able to handle pencils and other tools with increasing skill in the process of drawing, painting, modelling, printmaking, collage, textile and clay work and begin to choose materials appropriate for their work.
Year 6	Pupils extend the variety, scope and content of their own work and have developed some skills in selecting and using equipment, materials and techniques in the process of drawing, painting, modelling, printmaking, collage, textile and clay work.
Knowledge	
Year 2	Pupils can begin to identify different kinds of art, craft and design and recognise that work comes from different times and places.
Year 4	Pupils can identify different kinds of art, craft and design and begin to recognise the materials and methods used by the artists. They begin to identify the characteristics of work from different periods, cultures and traditions.
Year 6	Pupils can identify the materials and methods used by artists, craftworkers and designers and can understand the outcomes have different purposes. They also know that works reflect different periods, cultures and traditions.
Understanding	
Year 2	They can describe works of art, craft and design, saying what they like or dislike about them and explaining why. They can begin to apply similar qualitative judgments in talking about their own work.
Year 4	They can demonstrate a broader perception of art, craft and design and use a developing specialist vocabulary to talk about them. They are more aware of their own strengths and weaknesses and this helps them to evaluate their own work.
Year 6	Pupils can use a speciaist vocabulary to talk about works of art, craft and design. They are able to make simple aesthetic judgments and can assess and improve their own work.

FIG 14.7
OFSTED 'Benchmarks' for art

Examples of descriptions of achievement

Key Stage 1	Key Stage 2
Record responses to direct experiences, memory and imagination	
Is beginning to use different media to make symbols to represent ideas and to make images from observation and memory	Is able to work independently, using a variety of media to record ideas from observation, memory and imagination and is using the visual elements of colour, pattern etc. competently
Is beginning to use some of the visual elements (line, colour, pattern etc.) to represent ideas and make images from observation and memory	Shows an awareness of how the visual elements of art can be used selectively to represent experience and ideas from observation and memory
Is showing an understanding of the visual elements of art and is using them positively to make images based upon memory and observation	Is using knowledge of the visual elements of art and can use them thoughtfully and selectively to record images and ideas both from observation and imagination
Review and modify their work as it progresses	
Is beginning to talk about work made	Can describe how work has been made and to what effect and can identify possible improvements
Can describe how work has been made and how materials and techniques have been used	Will talk confidently about how work has been made and can identify how it can be improved and developed in future work in art
Will comment upon how work has been made and will suggest improvements	Is able to reflect upon, evaluate and modify work made and has good ideas about how work might be developed in the future
Respond to and evaluate different kinds of art including their own and other's work	
Can describe and see some connections between their own work and that of others	Can describe how they have used reference to other artists' work to develop ideas for their own work and make some use of an art vocabulary to justify opinions about work
Is beginning to make use of other artists' methods in their own work and can describe their own likes and dislikes in art	Is using art language competently to consider and compare their own work and that of others and is making thoughtful reference to other artists' work in support of their own making
Is beginning to make use of an art vocabulary to explain their preferences in art — can explain what they have learnt from other artists' work	Is confident and articulate in using an art language to justify and evaluate their own work and has made positive use of other artist's work in developing ideas for making different kinds of art

FIG 14.8
Descriptions of achievement

Transferring information to secondary schools

The effective transfer of information about children's work to colleagues in secondary schools can play an important part in developing continuity and progression in the teaching of art and design. Traditionally, many art teachers in secondary schools have tended to assume that children coming to them at eleven plus have had little or no art and design education in their primary schools — despite the fact that, at whatever level, the children will have been at least drawing and painting regularly for six years!

National Curriculum developments have necessarily given a sharper focus to the transition between key stages and have, at least, provided colleagues in secondary schools with the accepted framework for the teaching of art and design in Key Stages 1 and 2.

There are a number of ways in which information about children's progress and achievements in art can usefully be transferred to secondary schools. Some of these will be determined by transfer policies agreed between secondary schools and their neighbouring primary schools.

Assessment profiles

Assessment profiles, similar to those designed for reporting to parents can provide a useful summary of children's experience to colleagues in secondary schools.

Portfolios

Primary schools can transfer to secondary schools a small portfolio (say six to eight items) of work made by the children during years 5/6. The children themselves might be involved in the selection of which items of work they would like to go forward to their new schools.

Sketchbooks

The child's last sketchbook from their primary school, would make a very valuable transfer document, as it will give colleagues in senior schools a very useful starting point for discussion with their new students about their work and ideas.

Other useful forms of liaison might include providing secondary schools with a checklist of which artists, craftworkers and designers have been studied by the children in Years 5 and 6, so that colleagues can build upon work in critical studies undertaken in Key Stage 2 and take it forward in Key Stage 3.

The most useful form of liaison is, of course, to find opportunities to work with colleagues in the secondary sector. Opportunities for sharing experiences of children's art at both stages can be arranged during the school year.

Art and design teachers in secondary schools are very experienced in moderating and assessing children's work at 16 plus through their work for GCSE and A level over many years. Many might welcome the opportunity to share with you and your colleagues a session where you are reviewing children's work towards the end of Key Stage 2 so that they can both contribute to the debate and become better informed about the level of children's achievements at 11 plus.

Such exchange of information between teachers working in Key Stages 2 and 3, and such sharing of work, can only support and benefit the progression that children make in their work in art and design and may go some way towards ensuring that the work they have undertaken in their primary schools is used as an effective foundation for further achievements later in their schooling.

Useful references

SCAA (1996) *Consistency in Teacher Assessment: Exemplification of Standards in Art, Key Stage 3* (London: HMSO ISBN 1 85838 117 7)

OFSTED (1995) *Art: A Review of Inspection Findings, 1993/1994* (London: HMSO ISBN 0 11 350059 9)

Part five Resources for learning

Chapter 15
Resources and suppliers

Resources and suppliers

Many LEAs have produced documents to support their schools in developing schemes of work. If your own LEA has done so there should already be a copy in your school.

Below is an example of a scheme of work that offers guidance about progression, content and possible structure, without being narrow and prescriptive.

Copies can be ordered from the Wirral and are available to teachers outside the LEA if you telephone the given number.

Scheme of Work for Art, 1995
Metropolitan Borough of Wirral
Tel: 0151 6662121

Reference is made to other LEA schemes in the handbook and it is well worth approaching the Chief Education Office of the appropriate LEA to ask whether their schemes are generally available.

Equipment

The following gives specific guidance for the range of equipment you will need (This includes suggestions for both key stages).

Drawing/Mark making

Pencils, large drawing
Pencils, HB
Pencils, 2B
Pencils, 4B
Pencils, 6B
Charcoal
Chubbie Stumps
Crayola
Chalks
Craypas (oil pastels)
Chalk pastels

Pens
Fibre/felt tip pens
A range of drawing and
writing inks

Brushes
Nylon brushes size 4
Nylon brushes size 6
Nylon brushes size 8
Nylon brushes size 10
Nylon brushes size 12
Nylon brushes size 2
Decorators' brushes 25mm

Painting

Powder colour
Water based printing inks
Acrylic paints
All in the following colours:

Warm blue
Bright red

Lemon yellow
Ochre yellow
Burnt umber
Black
White } plenty
Crimson red
Mixing palettes
Water pots, powder pots

Paper

Newsprint (kitchen paper)
Black sugar
White sugar
Off white sugar
Assorted (subtle) colours, sugar
Cartridge paper
A4 duplicating paper

White cartridge
Water colour paper
Thin and thick card
Strawboard
Tissue paper (plenty of white
and some colours)
Coloured foil paper
Drafting paper

3D work and collage

Glue (PVA)
Wallpaper paste
Mod roc
Wire
Wire cutters
Masking tape

Jugs
Sieve
Sponges
Modelling tools
Plasticene
Sand

Newspaper

Clay

Rolling pins

Playdough (?)

Chicken wire

Brown gummed paper

Print making

Water-based inks as above

Rollers

Trays

Found objects

Combs

Polystyrene tiles

Lino tiles

Lino tile cutters

Textiles

Thrums

Wool

Twine

Jute

Sewing thread

Silks

Assorted needles

Scissors

Bodkins

Cold water dyes and fix

Easibrush or brusho

Hessian

Calico

Cotton

Jute

Scrim

Thick card

Small weaving frames/+ large
if possible

Drawing pins

Trigger tacker

Shared equipment

Camera

Batik pot(s)

Wax

Staple gun and staples

Kiln

Paper trimmer

Photocopier

Sewing machine

Iron

Ironing board

Collections

Post cards

Objects for observational drawing

Posters
Newspaper
Magazines

IT equipment and CD Rom: This is an ever changing area but you need packages which cover
a) graphics manipulation/draw type
b) creative — Paint type
c) CD Rom — Art Gallery type

Material suppliers

Contact

Potclays Limited
Brick Kiln Lane   – Quality clay and fast delivery
Etruria
Stoke-on-Trent
ST4 7BP
Tel: 01782 219816
Fax: 01782 286506

Most LEAs have their own suppliers.

Cheshire County Council Pisces
Central Stores   Westwood Studios,
Picow Farm Road   West Ave.,
Runcorn   Crewe,
Cheshire   Cheshire CW1 3AD
WA7 4UB   Tel: 01270 216211
Tel: 01928 580975

Specialist Crafts Limited Alexander Paper Supplies
PO Box 247   Dagfields Craft Centre,
Leicester   Crewe Rd.,
LE1 9QS   Walgherton,
Tel: 0116 251 0405   Nr. Nantwich,
                           Cheshire, CW5 7LG
                           Tel: 01270 842021

Yorkshire Purchasing Company
41 Industrial Park   – Fast delivery, excellent quality
Wakefield
WF2 0XE

Galleries and museums

Using Art Galleries with Children

Remember that on all trips you are responsible for the children's safety and well being. Ensure an adequate ratio of adults to children — for young children this ought to be one adult to two children. Even with older children you may well maintain this ratio for particular trips e.g. one adult cannot adequately supervise and discuss with eight children at Eureka! Science Museum. The children should not be left to wander — you should not take risks with other people's children!

On your preliminary visit consider the following:

Access
Is there an encouraging entry to the building?

There will be security at / in the entrance — there to ensure security of the artefacts — warn the children of this and discuss with gallery staff — some children could find the close presence of an officious security guard frightening. Equally the presence of security guards at the entrance should not give rise to a false sense of security on your behalf with regard to the safety of the children — you are responsible for their personal safety at all times.

Consider the atmosphere of the gallery — akin perhaps to that of a library — other people will probably be visiting whilst your class is there — the children will need to know about appropriate behaviour. You could usefully discuss any preconceptions the children may have about galleries prior to the visit.

To what extent are the possibilities of touching artefacts clearly signalled to the children — do they need to be able to read 'don't touch' signs? Could your rule be that they must ask the adult they are with first?

Language
Pick up enough plans of the gallery for at least each adult accompanying the children — highlight particular exhibitions to be studied and meeting places.

Look at the labelling and consider how appropriate it is for your children — either prepare the children so that they can read / recognise the signs and / or prepare the adults accompanying the children for the fact that they will have to be talking signs. Do the labels make use of figurative elements — these will help readers and non-readers alike and a gallery which has provided these is really trying to encourage good communication.

Understanding and appreciation

To what extent does the gallery provide a context for the artefact or the exhibition through the labelling provided. What is the narrative in, say, the picture? You will need to know a great deal about the context of abstract art to really be able to understand it and use it with the children.

Galleries may offer some or all of the following

education officer

school visits

family fun days

week-end and holiday extended hours for parents to bring children e.g. the Whitworth offers 'Mischief Makers' during the holidays

pre-visit preparation sessions for teachers

teachers' twilight sessions relating to the displays — e.g. talk by curator/education officer responsible

children may be invited to select work for exhibition from gallery stores

workshops for children with artists

Art reflects our history — times, sensibilities and economic pressures. When you are looking at artefacts:

1. What do you see? (description)
2. How are things put together? (analysis)
3. What is the artist trying to say? (interpretation)
4. What do you think of it? (judgment)

I would suggest that for most of us there is usually an initial step missing from the above which is the immediate — knee jerk — response of first impression. Often we either like something or we don't immediately — what you need to develop for yourself and your children is the ability to look, notice, consider meaning, reflect and describe / articulate your response.

Adapted from Gaitskell and Hurwitz, 1970, ref in Barnes, R. 1989.

The following have education programmes as well as rich and varied collections. A short list is given, but you need to research your own area as suggested in Chapter 1.

The Art Directory (Julian Homer, 1993) is an invaluable source of information.

Bury Art Gallery
Moss Street
Greater Manchester
Tel: 0161 705 5879

Oldham Art Gallery
Union Street
Oldham
Greater Manchester
Tel: 0161 678 4653

Whitworth Art Gallery
University of Manchester
Oxford Road
Manchester
Tel: 0161 273 4865

Tate Gallery Liverpool
Albert Dock
Liverpool
Tel: 0151 709 3223

Merseyside Maritime Museum
Albert Dock
Liverpool
0151 207 0001

The British Museum
Great Russell Street
London
WC1B 3DG
Tel: 0171 636 1555

Tate Gallery
Millbank
London
SW1P 4RG
Tel: 0171 821 1313

National Portrait Gallery
St Martin's Place
London
WC2H 0HE
Tel: 0171 306 0055

Sheffield Graves Art Gallery
Surrey Street
Sheffield
Tel: 01742 734 781

Birmingham Museum and Art Gallery
Chamberlain Square
Birmingham
Tel: 0121 235 2834

Oxford Ashmolean Museum
Beaumont Street
Oxford
OX1 2PH
Tel: 01965 278018

References

BARNES, R. (1989) *Art, Design and Topic Work*, London: Routledge.

BOWDEN, J. (1996) *Writing an Art Policy and Curriculum Plan for a Primary School*, London: AAIAD.

CLARKE, R. (1995) 'A Guide for Student Art Coordinators, (unpublished) Lancaster: University College of St. Martins.

CLEMENT, R. (1993) *The Readiness of Primary Schools to Teach the National Curriculum in Art*, Plymouth: University of Plymouth.

CLEMENT, R. (1993) *The Art Teacher's Handbook: Second Edition*, Cheltenham: Stanley Thornes.

CLEMENT, R. and PAGE, S. *Principles and Practice in Art*. Essex: Oliver and Boyd.

CLEMENT, R. and PAGE, S. (1992) *Knowledge and Understanding in Art*, Essex: Oliver and Boyd.

CLEMENT, R. and PAGE, S. (1994) *Primary Art, Essex:* Oliver & Boyd.

CLEMENT, R. and TARR, E. (1992) *A Year in the Art of a Primary School*, Wiltshire: NSEAD.

DFE (1992) *Art for Ages 5 to 14*, London: HMSO.

HOMER, J. (1993) *The Art Directory*, London: Macmillan.

KELLOGG, R. (1969) *Analysing Children's Art*, National Press Books, California, USA.

MORGAN, M. (1988) *Art 4/11*, Oxford: Blackwell.

OFSTED (1995) *Art: A Review of Inspection Findings*, London: HMSO.

PIOTROWSKI, J. (1991) 'Non-chronological writing at Key Stage Two', *Primary English*, vol. 2.

PIOTROWSKI, J. (1992) 'Contemporary issues in early years education', *Education 3–13 Journal*, Spring 1993.

PIOTROWSKI, J. (1994) 'Art for everyone's sake', in HARRISON, M. (Ed) Beyond the Core, Northcote House.

PIOTROWSKI, J. (1995) 'Coordinating Art', in HARRISON, M. (Ed) *Coordinating the Primary Curriculum at Key Stage Two*, London: Falmer Press.

PIOTROWSKI, J. (Ed) (1996) *The Expressive Arts in the Primary School, Special Needs in Ordinary Schools*, London: Cassell.

PIOTROWSKI, J. (1996) 'Art for all', in PIOTROWSKI, J. (Ed) The Expressive Arts in the Primary School, London: Cassell.

PIOTROWSKI, J. and RAY, R. (1993) 'Foundation subject: Art', in PUMFREY, P. and VERMA, G. (Eds) *Cultural Diversity and the Curriculum*, Vol. 3, London: Falmer Press.

SCAA (1995) *Planning the Curriculum at Key Stages 1 and 2*, London: HMSO.

SCAA (1996) *Consistency in Teacher Assessment. Exemplification of Standards in Art, Key Stage 3*, London: HMSO.

SCAA (1997) *Expectations in Art at Key Stages 1 and 2*, London: HMSO.

SCDC (1990) *The Arts 5–16, Practice and Innovation*, Essex: Oliver and Boyd.

STEPHENS, K. (1994) *Learning Through Art and Artefacts*, London: Hodder and Stoughton.

TAYLOR, R. (1986) *Educating in Art*, Harlow: Longman.

TAYLOR, R. (1992) *Visual Arts in Education*, London: Falmer Press.

TTA (1996) *Consultation Paper on Standards and a National Professional Qualification for Subject Leaders*, London: HMSO.

Index